JESUS
The Man of PRAYER

JOHN HENRY STRONG

. . . has climbed the high mountains of the world

JESUS
The Man of PRAYER

By JOHN HENRY STRONG

Philadelphia
THE JUDSON PRESS
Los Angeles   Chicago

To my father

AUGUSTUS HOPKINS STRONG

From whose rectitude, wisdom, stalwart faith

and tender love

I still draw heavenly inspiration

CONTENTS

CONTENTS

Jesus: Our Authority and Example in Prayer

"Men ought always to pray and not to faint."

Luke 18:1

"Ask, and it shall be given you; seek, and ye shall find; knock, and it shall be opened unto you."

Luke 11:9

"If ye abide in me, and my words abide in you, ask whatsoever ye will, and it shall be done unto you."

John 15:7

I

Have more people than ever before been praying in this epoch of world agony? Who can tell us? The Gallup Poll has not yet tiptoed into the realm of the spiritual.

Certainly more people than ever before might have been praying. The religion of Christ, together with the Bible which documents it, has within the last generation been planted inside the borders of every remaining non-Christian land, so that prayer as a resource and prayer as a weapon has within our time been within the reach of more human beings than ever before since the Christian message was first proclaimed twenty centuries ago. Never before in history have so many heard the words:

"Ask, and it shall be given you; seek, and ye shall find; knock, and it shall be opened unto you."[1]

Or those other words:

"If ye abide in me, and my words abide in you, ask whatsoever ye will, and it shall be done unto you."[2]

More people than ever before should have been praying. The issues at stake have been vaster. They have touched more people. It has not been a matter of rationed food or mounting taxes. It has not been that the sum total of human anguish suffered in our day has surpassed that suffered by any preceding generation. It has not been even that uncounted millions of the world's magnificent youth have marched straight to their graves, nor has it been the oceans of grief they have left behind. For these are not final, unconquerable ills. No one who has found sweet-

11

ness hidden in adversity, or known the ecstasy of sacrifice, or glimpsed beyond the losses of this present world another and a better world to which this is but the antechamber, can ever appraise catastrophe, suffering, or even death itself as irremediable loss.

But there have been other evils, more insidious and ominous by far, stalking the earth. Cruelty, lust, falsehood, pride and hate have trampled underfoot all that humanity by faith and martyrdom have won. On an English liner in 1939, an intelligent refugee just escaped from Germany, said, "Of all the evils the Nazis have inflicted on our nation, nothing equals the destruction of our moral integrity." If destruction like this conquers in the end, there will emerge upon this planet a life destitute of honor, virtue, and reverence for human kind, and society will sink to a leaden composite of masters and slaves. The slaves will beg for death. The masters—worse fate—will die of degeneration.

Never since Bethlehem has spiritual antagonism been etched so black against the sky. Never since Golgotha have light and darkness so joined in death grapple. We who have stood watching an old world die, and a new one in the pains of birth — what will happen to us, if we do not pray?

The grimness of life in such a world puts priceless value on encouragements to pray. These are not wanting. Philosophy seems weary of materialism. Science begins to discover within the seen and temporal the unseen and eternal.

Soldiers lost in the jungles or adrift on the Pacific have been given eye-opening deliverances while praying. Cast into the same crucible of suffering, Catholics, Jews

and Protestants have clasped hands.* Something today
has been lifting casual conversations up to spiritual levels
and swelling the tide of churchgoers. An awareness, as of
a brooding Presence, answering to human need and
responsive to faith, is widely witnessed to in popular maga-
zines and challenging editorials. The world, shipwrecked
on God, seems on the brink of prayer.

On the brink, not closer. Prayer is not rooted spon-
taneously and firmly in the thought and life of our generation. When I lived in New England, they used to tell me
that we were living on the prayers of our grandfathers.
Preachers, they said, used to make God seem big as they
have not since. The keynote of our age is UTILITY, and
the means by which it is pursued emphasizes a class of
aptitudes and instruments entirely different from those
which avail in the prayer-life. Prayer, in the ordinary
view, is not essential to, or even related to, the processes
of buying and selling, trying cases, curing patients, raising
crops or teaching pupils. Prayer as energy, prayer as light,
prayer as adjustment to the tasks and burdens of life,
prayer as unsealer of the fountains of hope — most of all,
prayer as achiever of concrete changes in the world of men
and of things, is no *indigene,* to use a biological word, in
the crash and confusion of the world today. To quote a
writer whose style is as rippling as his skepticism is corro-
sive, "Prayer is painting your wishes against the clouds.
When they happen true, you call it answered prayer. When
they don't, you call it submission to the Almighty."†

* A troopship was torpedoed in the Atlantic. In the confusion four soldiers
lost their life belts. Four chaplains—a rabbi, a Catholic, and two Protestants—
removed their own life belts and fastened them on the soldiers. They were last
seen kneeling on the deck in prayer, clasping one another's hands, as the ship
disappeared and the four soldiers floated off to safety.

† Freely quoted from Santayana, *Reason in Religion,* pp. 40-43.

Prayer means time. Prayer means detachment. Prayer means emancipation from environment and habit. People do not learn to pray unless taught by some commanding example or forced by some eye-opening discipline. We might wonder that so many pray. And how we need to ask,

"Lord, teach us to pray, as John also taught his disciples."[3]

Sad indeed is the case of those who, religiously reared, are spiritually adrift; who prayed once, but pray no longer. Gifted often, aglow with unselfish service, yet isolationist to all higher control, they are as unalert to a contiguous, heavenly world as blind Bartimæus was before the power of Christ touched him. Who will bestow on personalities like these the only life there is, which dawns when faith dawns and the Spirit of prayer and supplication[4] descends upon us?

No, this is not a praying, but an unbelieving, frightened and mad world. Pessimism infects men's sober judgments. Fear tosses them like the waves of the sea. As one and the same sun softens the wax but hardens the clay, so the same trouble humbles one and infuriates another. The dread surgery to which divine providence unwillingly resorts to shock the world awake and incline it to do justly, love mercy, and walk humbly with God, serves with many as the buttress of atheism and an invitation to moral surrender. So war wages are squandered on baubles, leisure on flimsy "best sellers" and profane melodrama, and leaning hard on alcohol, men add their bit to the degeneration of the times.

No doubt we have our better moments. Who, listening in a susceptible mood to someone praying, has not caught a tremor of contrition, a flash of certitude, or a sob of brokenhearted surrender, that has shattered self-complacency and commanded in terms not to be gainsaid,

"Put off thy shoes from off thy feet, for the place whereon thou standest is holy ground"?[5]

A man I know was praying aloud in a rescue mission. A lawyer entered, exuberant, carefree and self-sufficient. But as he heard my friend pray, something happened. A door was swung open as by invisible hands. The eyes of his heart were enlightened. He was ushered into an unimagined and new spiritual world. In a single instant,

"Old things are passed away; behold, all things are become new."[6]

Readers of Plato never fail to delight in the skill with which Socrates elicited from his adoring pupils the self-evident truth that the right person from whom to learn the art of carpentering is the carpenter and not the musician, and the right person from whom to learn the art of shoe-making is the shoemaker and not the shipwright. For it is only the specialists that teach us; and to whom among these do we turn supremely for light on the most indispensable of all the arts, the art of praying, but to him of whom it is written that

"As he prayed, the fashion of his countenance was altered, and his raiment was white and glistening"?[7]

Mortal man may no longer hear Jesus pray, yet his prayers survive in the Memoirs we call the Gospels, to search, shame, and recreate us. Reinforced by invitations, stern commands and unlimited promises, the prayers of Jesus discover to us the wellspring of his wisdom and power, the soul of his method, and the root and recipe of all life lived under the smile and by the power of God.

In every great crisis of his life, we find that Jesus prayed. But these crises, it is very important to observe, were not grafted on life from some alien source, but are typical of the crises through which all spiritual life passes and upon which all enduring character is built.

First of all, as Jesus passed through the door of baptism into the joy, peace and power of the public ministry, and into its blood, sweat and tears also, he prayed the Prayer of Self-dedication. When he stood on the verge of vital decisions, or negotiated his inevitable load of disappointment, weariness and depression, he prayed the Prayer of Dependence. When he foresaw his disciples tottering on the edge of moral precipices, he prayed the Prayer of Intercession. When bright angels descended from heaven bearing victorious answers to his supplications, he prayed the Prayer of Thanksgiving. When in the Garden, exposed to the sharpest darts the great adversary could hurl against him, till even the face of the Father dimmed, and the everlasting arms which had always supported him seemed to loosen, he prayed the Prayer of Submission. And when there was no immediate good in sight to be asked and no dire evil threatening to be delivered from, and Jesus simply sought, found and rested in the bosom of his Father, he prayed the Prayer of Fellowship and Communion.

So Jesus' whole life was a prayer. But if the life of Jesus was a prayer, then the life of the Christian must be prayer and all that comes out of prayer. We may let the last haunting doubt concerning prayer's rationality or efficacy vanish when Jesus bids us pray, for the inmost secret of the most perfect of all lives was not rooted in ecclesiastical dogma, or in speculation, or in wishful thinking, but in *competence based on perfect experience.* Jesus never said,

"Understand prayer" — that would have left us with a problem rather than with a duty. He says, "Pray." Jesus ranges behind prayer as surely as behind immortality all the splendor of his own moral integrity when he says to his followers,

"If it were not so, I would have told you."[8]

I was stalled in naturalism once. The developmental order, the chain of cause and effect, the normal sequences and cosmic regularities, controlled my thinking. But when by God's grace I was enabled to know him, the limitations prescribed by the lower, structural order of things ceased to dominate. I found myself in a universe of personalities, and personality has its own laws and regularities — laws of will, of relationship, of harmony and response. I came to see that love is a law, and pity a law, and mercy a law, and forgiveness of repentant sinners a law, and divine fidelity a law, and overflowing readiness to supply a law, and readiness to create all that is needful a law. These, I came to realize, are the immutable laws, while the regularities which we discern, infer, measure, and are prone to extol, are no more than the visible and partial mechanism for their realization.

"The heavens are the works of thy hands. They shall perish . . ."[9]

Like the prophet, I saw a *spirit in the wheels,* guiding them, checking them, perchance even halting them — in any event gloriously using them for the fulfilling of the prayers of the Christian and the accomplishment of the purposes and promises of God.

So I found myself no longer scandalized by the idea of a "supernatural world." For what did the words cover?

Simply that higher order of things, that world of supersensible fact, into which I make incursions by love, faith and prayer, and in whose treasures I share by the payment of a spiritual price. I do not share in the treasures of the lower, structural, visible order in that way. I do not get the air I breathe that way. The farmer pays no spiritual price for sunshine. God makes his sun to rise on the evil and on the good, and sends his rain on the just and on the unjust, whether they pray or do not pray. But there are blessings within human reach which do not come in that same free way. To get the joy of forgiveness, courage to battle on, light on my way, power to rescue a soul from the powers of darkness, I must do something. I must humble myself, call on God, and hold on by faith and prayer — I must pay a spiritual price. When I pay the price they come. When I do not, they do not come. Love, faith, prayer, become causes, as it were, drawing down light and life from the higher, supersensible world. That higher world does not violate or infringe upon the ordinary world of my common experiences — it permeates it, takes it up into itself, completes and glorifies it. There is harmony between the two. There is also difference, and it is quite as important to maintain the difference as the harmony. I must not, in the supposed interests of simplicity, blot out the line between the natural and supernatural. When I do so, I not only ignore the universe's higher order, richness and variety, but I virtually tell others that forgiveness and courage, infallible guidance and salvation, will drop down on men from the skies whether they pray or do not pray, whether they pay the price or do not pay the price. But they will not, and that is the tragedy of today. Stalled in the natural, men do not bow to the distinctness and supremacy of the supernatural. Their lives therefore are barren, and even their understanding of the physical world maimed and fragmentary, not being shot through with the radiance and rationality which spring from an experience of the divine through prayer.

It is as we pray, then, that we begin to understand. We begin then to wonder also, and to abase ourselves, and to praise, and to wield under safe inspiration powers "hid from the wise and understanding but revealed unto babes"; powers of enlightenment, of rehabilitation and redemption — powers that will yet bring heaven down to earth and establish a transformed humanity in a world free at last from the folly of war and the crime, shame and stain of sin.

Prayer and Life's Purpose:
The Prayer of Consecration

"Now when all the people were baptized, it came to pass, that Jesus also being baptized, and praying, the heaven was opened, and the Holy Ghost descended in a bodily shape like a dove upon him, and a voice came from heaven, which said, Thou are my beloved Son; in thee I am well pleased."

Luke 3:21-22

Here prayer emerges for the first time in the life-story of that Specialist in prayer, the Lord Jesus.

Measured by its importance, the reference seems brief, almost casual. Yet regarded as the first note of a melody and as a door to a life of prayer, the part serves well as sample of the whole, and barest mention suffices to put us in possession of what we need most to know—that when Jesus stood on life's threshold with the curtain down and all that was indispensable to him and to humanity unexperienced, unsuffered and undone, he prayed.

So, early in the Gospel story, foundations are laid for those who would follow in Christ's footsteps — for all who in this day of calamity and vast opportunity turn to prayer as heaven's gift and earth's most priceless treasure.

This is prayer's first emergence, not its beginning, in the life of Jesus. For that beginning one may search the Memoirs in vain. Who can ponder Jesus' words of wonder and protest when at the age of twelve he became separated from his parents at the feast in Jerusalem, was for three days painfully searched for, and finally found in the Temple:

"How is it that ye sought me? knew ye not that I must be in my Father's house?"[1]

and not see shining in them the light that must have shone from the lad's face as he spoke them—the serenity of a companionship with God as instinctive as breathing, and marking his whole self-conscious life from the beginning?

23

It was the very life and breath of Jesus to pray. It is doubtful if he ever knew a time when he did not pray.

But the years of childhood and youth, of self-discipline and waiting, were over, and a voice was heard from the wilderness summoning all Israel to repent, and proclaiming the speedy advent of the long-expected kingdom of God. One can almost see that kinsman of Jesus, John the Baptist—young, erect and stalwart, bronzed by the sun, with the eye of an eagle and a voice that rang through men's souls, opening chambers as it rang. Elijah the Second, Jesus later called him—"more than a prophet," greatest of all born of women.[2] He stood now on the banks of the Jordan where centuries before the nation had crossed into Canaan, and there called on all Israel to forsake the wilderness of disobedience and to pass once more through Jordan, but this time into a spiritual Canaan, registering its repentance in the cleansing of baptism.

Jesus had no sin to repent of, but in this universal summons which suffered no distinctions he heard the voice of God directing him to his lifework as Messiah of his people. He humbly presented himself for baptism with the multitude. He overruled the protest of the Baptist, "I have need to be baptized of thee, and comest thou to me?"[3] and as he was baptized he prayed. The sight of Jesus praying was not lost on John, himself a praying man, who had taught his disciples to pray.[4] He did not fail to note with keenest joy that this "Greater One," the latchet of whose shoes he was not worthy to unloose, assumed his task now as Sin-bearer and Saviour, not self-impelled, self-sufficient and alone, but as a suppliant, in conscious dependence, praying. Treasuring the sight, the Baptist shared it with others; for Luke, the historian, who in his

Gospel has more to say about prayer than any other evangelist, came upon it in his wide and painstaking researches and enshrined it for us there forever.

So prayer appears for the first time in the life-story of Jesus. We should like to know the words of this prayer, but they are withheld from us. We are the poorer for this. Of what value is it to know that Jesus prayed, if we may not know what he prayed?

Yet silence may prove golden. Men have written books on the silences of Scripture. They have found them rich in suggestion, and have listed them among the assets of the Christian. Need this "silence," I ask, register a *purposed reticence?* Must it be likened to an armed angel set to rebuke presumption and to hide from us heavenly thoughts and holy desires which that day the ear of the Almighty alone was qualified to hear? May it not stand as an invitation, as a beckoning Providence, luring us to intensive thought and spiritual discovery?

But first let us not miss the values wrapped up in knowing that when Jesus was baptized, he prayed, even if we should know nothing more. Certainly the sight of perfect character linking itself with heaven by means of prayer did something for the Forerunner that day, even if the lips that prayed moved inaudibly. But something else was done by this adding of prayer to baptism, something bearing on the nature of true religion and the future of the Christian Church. A blow was struck that day at ritualism. An ordinance of the Church was lifted clean out of the category of the mechanical and formal and made a glowing act and expression of spirit. Nor was even that all. How much we owe to Jesus' prayer at his baptism as a reminder that the time of all times to pray is on life's threshold. Not after we have tried and failed, and life's bloom is off, and God looms before the soul as a possible last resort, but in life's magic dawn, when all Nature wears a halo, and Hope is boundless, and the soul is charged with the romance and glory of life's first beginnings—that is the time of times to pray!

And so I come to Jesus' baptismal prayer. I feel as Moses must have felt when he stood before the burning bush and heard God say, "Put off thy shoes from off thy feet, for the place whereon thou standest is holy ground."[5] May the temper of the Psalmist be mine when he said, "My soul cleaveth unto the dust: quicken thou me according to thy word."[6] For how can earth-gravitating, sin-blunted minds like ours attain to the clarity or the humility which he must possess who would discern the unvoiced thoughts of the Son of God? But there is a Spirit of God, who alone "searcheth . . . the deep things of God."[7] He "is no respecter of persons."[8] He takes the things of Christ and shows them to us, and I feel his need the more that the door at which I knock is ajar, and unquestioned light is streaming through.

For is not the door ajar? Open the Gospels, and it is not Christ's reticences but his confidences that meet you, the disclosures he makes, the secret things he reveals.

"No longer do I call you servants; for the servant knoweth not what his lord doeth: but I have called you friends; for all things that I have heard from my Father I have made known unto you."[9]

Jesus stands at the door and knocks, asking and offering intimacy.[10] He bestows a mystic "white stone" on all who overcome, and on it "a new name written, which no man knoweth but he that receiveth it."[11] The summit of self-bestowal seems reached when we discover that Jesus does not hide even his prayers from us. For he knows nothing of that constraint which we so often feel when we try to pray before others, and which we camouflage as "reticence" when we do not praise it as virtue. Concealment in what is sacredly personal is not part and parcel of the perfection of our great High Priest, mediator between earth and heaven. Ten times in Luke's Gospel I find Jesus praying in the presence of others. In five of these he turns from communion with men to communion with God with all the unconsciousness of a child, and these include prayers which Christians hold the most sacred of all—the prayers in the Garden and from the Cross. Obviously, we must rediagnose this "reticence" and brand it the spiritual unreality it really is. God is not real to us and people are: hence our constraint. That is a lesson our soldiers in action have pressed upon us, for they have found that when God becomes more indispensably real than people, habits, and everything else, men pray with perfect abandon in the presence of others.

If now it appears at least fairly plausible that the baptismal prayer of Jesus may have been withheld to stimulate our surmises, and to enable us perhaps even to divine it, let us go back once more to the Jordan and listen to Jesus and to John. "I have need to be baptized of thee, and comest thou to me?" the Forerunner protests. "Suffer it now:" Jesus replies, "for thus it becometh us to fulfil all righteousness."[12] There, in one comprehensive, commanding word Jesus lays bare the direction of his mind, the quintessence of his desires, the secret of his life. Life's purpose is one thing and one only, self-identification with the purpose of him who sent him. Never before or since were reason and will, imagination and affection, so irrevocably laid on the altar of God's good, acceptable and perfect service. Jesus violates neither personal inclination nor ethical propriety when he is baptized alongside the sinful multitude—he is "the friend of publicans and sinners."[13] "Holy, harmless, undefiled, separate" from them he is, but he must be "numbered with the transgressors."[14] He must do in symbol what he has come to do in reality—incorporate himself with corrupt, guilty, lost mankind—shouldering its burden, consenting to its liabilities, bowing even to the graceless death which it will in due time deal out to him as his reward, and which baptism beneath Jordan's flood typifies. And the prayer of the hour? Can it be alien to the act? Manifestly, it must reflect and complete the act, and offer it as adoration to the Father.

The soul and substance of Jesus' baptismal prayer, then, can hardly remain longer in doubt. It is his Prayer of Consecration, of Self-dedication to the plan and will of God. The inaugural day has dawned, anticipated from the hour when his unique relationship to the Father first flashed on him and flooded the Scriptures concerning him with light. Jesus stands before the door which God has opened and no man can shut. "The light which lighteth every man" is about to spread. The Gospel is about to be given. As a Son, Jesus goes forward to manifest the Father; as a Lamb, to take upon him the sin of the world. And, as we see him praying, is it just fancy and nothing more, to recall another royal scene, and catch the echoes of a prayer uttered by Israel's anointed king centuries before, on a day of like consecration? The fortieth Psalm preserves it. Its words, noble on the lips of any monarch, seem in their implications less appropriate actually to David than prophetically to David's greater Successor:

"Lo, I come: in the volume of the book it is written of me, I delight to do thy will, O my God: yea, thy law is within my heart."[15]

Now we are not unaware of the vital role which David's Psalms and prayers played in the life and experience of the Savior. They foretold his coming. They voiced his agony. They furnished the stair on which his soul mounted as he hung stretched upon the Cross. They foreshadowed his triumph and universal reign. When, then, we add to considerations like these the arresting fact that a New Testament writer, nearer to the fountain of inspiration than we, found in the words of the Psalm we have quoted, *the perfect image and reflection of Jesus' mind and mediatorial office,* does the chance seem remote that we may have in them not merely the soul and substance, but in part, perhaps, the very words of Jesus' baptismal prayer?[16]

If in these vital matters we have not gone entirely astray, where, I ask, lies the significance of Jesus' baptismal prayer for his friends and followers? For if Jesus is our example anywhere, it is here. Let the fact, then, be pressed home that what came first and foremost with him, comes late or last with us. Pledged though we are to imitate Christ in all his imitable perfections, we are prone to hold back the consecration of body and soul, might, mind and strength, and to make it a belated and reluctant gift, if, indeed, it is ever our gift at all.

And why? Well, the ecstasies of unlimited and irresponsible freedom have first to be explored. Wings have to be tried—what else are wings for? Talents have to be buried, time squandered, plans wrecked, prayers resisted, hopes blasted, grace despised and suicidal folly demonstrated. Then perhaps some stern providence shipwrecks us on undeserved mercy, and we yield. We hand God a broken sword. We do what Jesus never needed to do—surrender.

Truly, we are mysteries crying aloud for diagnosis. We are a mystery, first, of ignorance. Had we not sinned and suffered enough to learn our dependence? Then why did we not make dependence complete and controlling? Had we never heard Christ's words, "Without me ye can do nothing?" Or were we stalwart exceptions, souls with immunities? Finer timber than the towering New Testament saint who cried: "For I know that in me (that is, in my flesh,) dwelleth no good thing"?[17]

But this is still skimming the surface. Why did we cherish our ignorance and find all self-scrutiny painful? Why did we cling to the illusion that a stronger self was bound to rise out of our unplumbed depths and elbow out of place the self that had played us false? Why, professing to believe in God, did we forget that there is room for but one God in the universe, and that sooner or later his will and way and not ours must prevail? And why, with the Father's tender face once for all unveiled in Christ, did we behave as though he were a tyrant jealous of our freedom and prepared to ordain for us sufferings and sacrifices which, if left free, we should never ordain for ourselves?

Veritable puzzles are we, yet not beyond analysis. Self-will had had a long running start with us. Enthroned since babyhood, it had been smiled on as innocence, praised as self-reliance, justified as self-protection and flattered as personality's central citadel. What wonder, then, if it clung fanatically to its poor pretense of power, averring that if permanent personal good was to be had at all, one must get it for one's self, and that a rich and a full life was un-

thinkable except as we "looked out for Number One."
We should spell "sin" with a capital "I." What wonder if,
having begun by deifying us, it ends by destroying us!

What wonder, too, that at last we grew suspicious of an
independence which had brought only disillusionment, and
though longing to yield to God, fell into self-distrust, won-
dering whether even a willing soul has within itself capacity
to dedicate itself as Jesus did. How much of an iceberg
is under water? How much of a ship? How much of a
proud building rests on foundations far out of sight? Is
not my mysterious self too vast to command? Can I perma-
nently deed my personality over to God as Jesus did? Will
not unsubdued regions mock at me as I try, and say,
"You'll find out soon enough how little of you has been
surrendered, and how much of you remains unconsecrated,
stubbornly and forever your own!"

Yet plainly the duty of the self-conscious fraction of a
man is to act for the whole. But can it? That troubled
me once, till I heard a godly man say, "Just as in writing
a book, an author sends copy to the printer as copy is
ready, and then more as more is prepared, so today I can
give to God all of myself I can gather up in one act of
will. God, the Searcher of hearts, will take the will for
the deed, and will give me grace, as unsurrendered depths
come to light, to bring them too into willing subjection."

Years ago one Sabbath afternoon I took two little children out into the woods. We had a confidential talk, and
at its close sat down on a log and prayed. Then I asked
them a question: "If you should look up and see Jesus
walking down the path toward us, what would you do?"

"We'd give him something," came the answer.

"What would you give him?"

"A piece of candy," said the littler one.

"Is there anything else you could give him?" I then asked.

And the older one answered, "I'd give him myself."

Years passed. Grown to manhood, and "facing the constant eyes of death," that child fulfilled the prophecy of those words; and as he gave himself fully and joyfully to Christ, Christ responded with a vision of himself such as has been vouchsafed to few of his saints. And is it not ever so? Alas, then, for our withholdings! Alas, for "the little rift within the lute"!

> "Oh, the little more, and how much it means;
> And the little less, and what worlds away!"

Yet when Christ has our all, there seems no limit to the divine bestowals. He girds himself to serve us. A nobler self rises from the altar on which our self-willed self was laid, and in our faint, human fashion we taste the glory with which the Father crowned the baptismal prayer of Jesus:

"The heaven was opened, and the Holy Spirit descended in a bodily form, as a dove, upon him, and a voice came out of heaven, Thou art my beloved Son; in thee I am well pleased."[18]

Prayer and Life's Demands:
The Prayers of Dependence

"And he continued all night in prayer to God. And when it was day, he called his disciples; and he chose from them twelve, whom also he named apostles."

Luke 6:12-13 (A. R. V.)

"And he healed many that were sick with divers diseases. . . . And in the morning, a great while before day, he rose up and went out, and departed into a desert place, and there prayed."

Mark 1:34-35 (A. R. V.)

3

I HAVE spoken of the first recorded prayer of Jesus, the prayer which he offered as he passed through the door of baptism into his public ministry—his Prayer of Self-dedication, his Prayer of Consecration to his Father's plan and will. I turn now to the prayer which Jesus offered when he found himself on the verge of momentous decisions; the prayer also which he offered when burdened with weariness and disappointment, and when threatened with defeat—his Prayer of Dependence. I shall call this chapter Prayer and Life's Demands.

What are the demands which life makes upon one? They are many, and I mention only three of them. First, life's great decisions must be correct decisions and life's great choices, wise choices. Second, one must be prepared and willing to pay the full price in weariness, disappointment, opposition, and if need be, defeat, in fulfilment of the purpose to which life has been dedicated. Third, since such demands as these overpass the natural powers of un-aided flesh and blood, one must learn the art and establish the habit of tapping those heavenly reservoirs of wisdom and strength which are lavishly offered to faith and are available for human help.

1.

Take first the demand that life's great decisions should be correct decisions and life's great choices, wise choices. Surely Jesus never faced a more important decision, a more momentous choice, than in the choice of his twelve disciples. Any one familiar with the world of enterprise and administration knows that the success of the administrator depends not simply and solely on his own personal aptitudes and abilities, but quite as much if not more on his skill in selecting as subordinates men of talent and promise whom he can train, imbue with his own enthusiasm, and bind loyally to himself as with cords of steel.

Some years ago, I baptized into the Christian church a distinguished railroad man. He had started as a boy at the foot of the ladder and mounted to the top. He was responsible for everything that happened on the Union Pacific railroad from Kansas City at its eastern end to Portland and Los Angeles on the west—all the trackage, all the rolling stock, all the personnel and policies. The success of Carl R. Gray, however, was due, not simply to his experience in railroad affairs, his industry and his ability, but quite as much to an extraordinary skill that was his in reading human nature and attracting to himself as assistants men of great ability. Just to talk with these men was to sense at once their caliber and devotion.

Now our Lord's choice of his twelve disciples surpassed far in significance any railroad president's choice of his subordinates. Never had men been chosen for so exalted or for so exacting an office. Christ's enterprise was to touch the ends of the earth and the fate of all coming generations. The time allotted for the preparation of his followers for their task, also, was incomparably short. In four short years at most, our Lord's followers were to be bereft of his visible presence and plunged into the work of explaining and defending his Gospel, maintaining its purity, unfolding its implications, and guiding it through uncharted seas of misunderstanding and persecution. Who and where were men fit for such an undertaking? Such was Jesus' problem, and we are concerned to know how he faced it.

As the day drew near when the Twelve were to be chosen, what were the natural abilities—looking at things first from a purely human point of view—which our Lord was able to bring to his task of selection? There was, first of all, an incomparable insight into human nature, an unexampled power to read the characters of men at a glance.

One night a businessman of my home town brought home with him a friend to meet his new wife. When the guest left, his wife turned to him and said, "Have nothing to do with that man, or you'll regret it." Startled, he began to spread out his friend's services and philanthropies. "That may be," she replied, "but mark my words. You'll regret it." Within a few weeks this citizen was behind the bars of State's Prison. Strange power that, capable of startling manifestations, and as valuable as exceptional.

That Jesus possessed this power in the highest degree the Memoirs make clear on almost every page. In the second chapter of John's Gospel, I read that at the first Passover of his ministry—

"Many believed on his name, beholding his signs which he did. But Jesus did not trust himself unto them, for that he knew all men, and because he needed not that any one should bear witness concerning man; for he himself knew what was in man."[1]

At a glance Jesus discerned the rocklike faith hidden in Peter's volatile nature.[2] Another glance revealed to him the aspirations and hopes of Nathanael.[3] The eyes of Jesus penetrated to the evil and the good. He saw the corrupt desire behind the lustful look, the broken heart beneath the penitent tear, the will to despise and to crucify him behind the plaudits of the miracle-gaping mob. This power Jesus brought to his task of choosing.

There was a second unique ability also which Jesus at this important time had at his command. Dare I speak of our Lord's common sense? What we call common sense means often little more than fallible worldly wisdom. Will Witter, twice missionary to Assam, used to say, "The common sense of this world is the nonsense of heaven." Shall I say then that Jesus had *uncommon sense*—a perspicacity, a clear-eyed wisdom, a cloudless and unfailing native sagacity which was an indispensable asset for the task before him.

Jesus, for example, could scarcely have chosen for his twelve disciples a dozen millionaires. Wealth rears barriers more often than it levels them. It puts its possessors on guard against their fellows even when there is no pride of power to deny them the simple fellowships and normal social contacts of life. Besides, twelve evangelists clad in soft raiment and with gold and silver coin clinking in their purses could hardly communicate to the world at large correct ideas of the nature and goods of Christ's kingdom. Still less could they bear personal witness to the fact that God, the Father, who clothes the lilies and feeds the ravens, will feed and clothe his servants when, destitute of all human support, they venture forth on his business at his command. As a young Frenchman of what French Protestants call the "Church of the Captivity" in German concentration camps, said, "It is only when everything but God is gone that one learns that God alone is enough."

No more could Jesus, with this native sagacity at his command, pick for his subordinates twelve learned scholars with ponderous degrees after their names, men conspicuous for their attainments, but in whom humility and brotherhood were in danger of being swallowed up by intellectual pride. Great learning, even in sacred matters, can insulate its possessors from human need as effectively as can wealth. It can seat men on high balconies of observation where they do little for humanity but survey it, theorize over its problems, analyze its tears into sodium chloride and water, and explain away its sins, sorrows and follies.

A Salvation Army lass was testifying for her Master in a crowded passenger train. Approaching a very dignified gentleman, she ventured to say, "Sir, I hope you're a Christian." Startled, this man of dignity replied, somewhat naively, "Why, I am a theological professor." The simple girl, confused by those weighty words, laid an earnest hand on his arm and replied, "My brother, don't let that stand in your way!"

George Bernard Shaw was guilty of both wit and wisdom when he once remarked concerning himself that for a period of years his education had been interrupted by his schooling. Education often seems only to begin when one gets out into the school of life. Jesus was not indifferent to formal education. If Professor Ramsey, who knew so much about Palestine in our Lord's time, was correct, education among the Jews in Jesus' day compared quite favorably in things essential with what is known as popular education today. Though unencumbered with the technical training of the schools, our Lord's disciples were not illiterates. They knew the Scriptures too well for that. "He appointed twelve, that they might be with him, and that he might send them forth."[4] That was their real school, that their theological seminary, and what they had learned earlier from both father and mother at home and in the synagogue school was preparation for it.

But if Jesus could not choose twelve financiers or twelve savants to be the apostles of his church, still less could he choose a dozen social stars—the Palestinian "Four Hundred," who could only be contemptuous of the underprivileged, the simple folk whom Jesus sought, cultivated and loved. Jesus was not averse to the skills and delicacies of polite society. The spirit he breathed was the very soul of courtesy and urbanity. One finds nothing offensive or raw in the quality, talk or behavior of the men who companied with him. They bear all the hallmarks of the wellborn and wellbred.

So it would seem, then, as though Jesus had only to look within himself to find sure direction for the important choice before him. Pray? Why should he pray? Would not "uncommon sense" tell him the kind of disciples he needed, and would not infallible insight point them out to him? Surely, it was only a question whether they existed and were at hand. If there were such men, he would have them whether he prayed or not. If there were not, he was not responsible.

And what would they be like? "Blessed are the poor in spirit":[5] they would be humble, teachable men who, like little children, knew that they were nothing and that God was everything. They would be men who could grasp and sympathize with his aims and interpret them to the world without modification or addition. They would be close to life—men of toil, familiar with its burdens, pains and griefs. They would be men of character, capable of self-sacrifice. Above all, they would be godly men, with a capacity for faith; men who had learned the Old Testament Scriptures from both father and mother at home, knew the laws of God, and from their deepest hearts felt that these should prevail; men who, whatever their superficial blemishes and limitations, were from their mother's womb irrevocably faced towards the goal which God had once for all set before Abraham, their forefather, and Moses, their lawgiver, when he ordained Israel to be a nation and consecrated it to be the carrier of salvation to the world. They would be faulty, for they would be human. They might not have chosen one another if the choosing had been left to them. Andrew might have seemed colorless and ineffective to his brother Peter, and Peter spasmodic and undependable to Andrew. Thomas might have blackballed John as a dreamy mystic; and John, Thomas as a rationalist and incorrigible skeptic. All, perhaps, might have chosen Judas, for aptitudes on the surface, and not for the deeper-down potentialities which Jesus saw, and to which till the very end he made his fruitless appeal.[6]

So, making clairvoyant insight his mentor and native sagacity his guide, Jesus would choose. So saith "common sense." But what saith the Scripture?

"And it came to pass in these days, that he went out into the mountain to pray; and he continued all night in prayer to God. And when it was day, he called his disciples; and he chose from them twelve, whom also he named apostles: Simon, whom he also named Peter, and Andrew his brother, and James and John, and Philip and Bartholomew. . . ."[7]

Jesus prayed all night? That is a long time to pray, and longer still for one who never lapsed into wandering thoughts, who warned against meaningless repetitions, and who taught that to be prevailing, true prayer, inspired from above, must fasten itself tenaciously to the thing asked for, persist against all discouragements, and so finally

draw it forth out of the mists of possibility as by the creative power of faith.

But this is perplexing. Are we to understand that Jesus,
possessed of unique powers adequate to his task, renounced
their normal use and substituted prayer to God in its
place? Did gifts like these become foci of infection to
corrupt, instruments of temptation to mislead? Then why
such gifts at all? From confusion like this Jesus' own
words deliver us. He who threatened with terrific sternness
against burying one's talents, and warned that "to whom-
soever much is given, of him shall much be required,"[8]
could hardly now be found burying and abjuring respon-
sibility for his own. That Jesus made use of the extraordinary powers with which he was endowed, the records
plainly show; but here we stand on the verge of a deep
mystery. We have come within sight of the main mystery
of Jesus' life and the paradox of all godly living. Inde-
pendent and self-sufficient though Jesus appears, and God's
only-begotten Son though we know him to have been,
he was nevertheless human like ourselves, and because
human, dependent.

"The Son can do nothing of himself, but what he seeth the Father
doing: for what things soever he doeth, these the Son also doeth in
like manner. For the Father loveth the Son, and showeth him all
things that himself doeth: and greater works than these will he show
him, that ye may marvel". . . "As I hear, I judge" . . . "The words
that I say unto you I speak not from myself: but the Father abiding
in me doeth his works."[9]

Three miles off shore from my Larchmont home, I saw
the Victory Ships laden with munitions of war drop
anchor, halting their journey across the Atlantic. Were
they awaiting the rest of a convoy before launching forth
on their dread errand of justice and mercy? No, but

freighted with vast cargoes of steel and iron, their com-
passes had to be tested, adjusted and rendered seaworthy
before they dared to set sail. So it is only when, through
self-surrender and prayer to God, we have "put to death
our members," effectively neutralizing the ignorance and
self-will stored deep within us, that the gifts and powers
with which we have been endowed begin freely to function, and what we call ours becomes really our own.

We were climbing the Aiguilles Rouges, my Swiss guide
and I. We had no lantern. We needed none, for the moon
was shining brightly, illuminating the snowy peaks above
us, as in the very early morning we ascended the long,
sloping meadow, soft under foot, that leads up to the
rocks on which that splendid mountain, rust-red, favorite
of rock-climbers, is founded. Suddenly, Antoine, who was
leading the way, stopped, turned and said, "The moon is
shining, the stars are glistening, all the world's asleep, and
we walk in the light of God!" Yes, that "perfect gentle
knight, mediaeval saint, tremendous man of the mountains," as Antoine was first described to me by the one who
introduced us, was right. We walk in the light of God,
if we walk at all—if, roped to our heavenly Guide, we
ever reach the heights where God's thoughts are made
clear, and his great purpose for us and for mankind unfolds before us.

For forty-five years now, I have tried never to enter on
an important course or make an important decision without first making sure of the divine guidance, and the re-
turns have long been coming in. The reward of acting
under the divine direction and of being sure that one is
in accord with the divine will in what one undertakes,
is of incalculable value to a human life. If Jesus needed

to pray before important decisions, far more do we. That young woman needs God's light on whom she elects to marry; that young man, on the calling to which he is to consecrate his life. The prophet cries:

"O Lord, I know that the way of man is not in himself: it is not in man that walketh to direct his steps."[10]

But James, our Lord's own brother, adds:

"If any of you lacketh wisdom, let him ask of God, who giveth to all liberally and upbraideth not; and it shall be given him."[11]

2.

But before this discussion of Prayer and Life's Demands is finished, we must look further and see how Jesus negotiated the inevitable load of weariness, discouragement, antagonism and threatened defeat which he was destined to carry throughout his public ministry.

A Christian physician once confided to me that to his mind one assumption and one alone explained the earthly life of Jesus—his possession of a perfect human body. The idea is not without its attractiveness. A flawless body would seem a fit setting for the jewel of a flawless spirit—a body so fashioned, tempered and inwardly co-ordinated as to lift its possessor above needless strain, prove capable of supreme effort, and so become the ideal and perfect servant of its possessor. Two facts, however, must never be lost sight of: first, our Lord's veritable humanity; and second, the nature, magnitude and persistence of the burdens he bore.

Think first of his burdens. Take the program of a single day as Mark in his fourth and fifth chapters pictures it. Jesus starts the day unveiling in parables the principles of the kingdom of God, from a small boat in which he has taken refuge from the throng that in its zeal seems bent on crowding him into the lake. That is no brief, thirty-minute exposition of the "mysteries of the kingdom" to which Jesus wholeheartedly gives himself, for no sooner is it over, and he has bidden his disciples turn the prow of the boat toward the other side, than we see him fast asleep in the stern on a pillow, although a fierce storm is raging around him. "Carest thou not that we perish?" they cry, awaking him as the boat fills. Rising, Jesus rebukes the wind, and the sea becomes a calm.

But there is no rest waiting for Jesus in Decapolis, for a demoniac, his body gashed with stones, advances toward them as they disembark. Him Jesus heals. Then follows the stirring narrative of the demons, the swine, and their owners who, dead to all values but their own property, beg Jesus to depart out of their coasts. Returning to the other side, Jesus finds again the omnipresent multitude seeking him, and elbowing his way through it, a man with an agony in his heart, Jairus, whose daughter lies not far away at the point of death, whom Jesus would heal. But as they turn thither, a woman, sorely afflicted with hemorrhage, has with her last ounce of strength pressed through the on-moving crowd and touched the hem of Jesus' robe with the hope of healing. "Who touched me?" Absurd question to all but two in that eager, straining crowd. Yet power has gone forth from Jesus, and he must stop and administer to the spirit of this believing woman the cure already bestowed upon her body. With an encouraging word to the despairing Jairus, Jesus once more presses on, but the wails of hired mourners soon reinforce the word of the messengers—he has come too late! "She is not

dead, but sleepeth" is his reply. His words awaken only
scorn. But taking the child's parents and three of his disciples with him, he presses into the sickroom, and with a
word to the dead child, "Little girl, stand up!" Jesus
restores her alive to her parents. And so ends the record of
one day.

But is this the whole or a fraction of the story—a frame-
work at most for such soul-expenditure and suffering as
only a mind and heart like Christ's could undergo? The
pressure of sweating crowds; endless contact not only with
physical infirmity but with moral ugliness; misunder-
standings; the self-interest and apostasy of friends; the acid
of controversy; the venom of men faced toward evil and in
league with the powers of darkness, who see their standing
with the populace imperiled just in the measure that Jesus
succeeds—these all combine to build up a burden which
only he could understand whose soul was as gentle and
whose purpose to save was as hungry as Christ's.

We blithely skim the depths of disappointment hid in
the words: "When the Son of man cometh, shall he find
faith on the earth?"[12] We by-pass the tumultuous scenes
when Jesus' overcharged spirit vents itself in lamentation
and loud weeping. We forget the literal fact that Jesus at
the end died, not of wounds or disease or exhaustion but
of a broken heart. Yet, till the angel of death plucked
him out of the clutches of his enemies, Jesus proved more
than conqueror and surmounted every woe. How? By
placid nerves? By will-power? By full use of incomparable
human resources? No, but once more by prayer, the prayer
of humble dependence on God. So Mark, in a scene which
the world's greatest artists should have immortalized in
color, puts burden and heavenly resource in juxtaposition

when he described the populace of Capernaum gathered
at Jesus' door. We love to sing about it:

> "At even, ere the sun was set,
>   The sick, O Lord, around thee lay;
> Oh, in what divers pains they met!
>   Oh, with what joy they went away!"

Or in the evangelist's words:

"And he healed many that were sick with divers diseases, and cast
out many demons; and he suffered not the demons to speak, because
they knew him. And in the morning, a great while before day, he
rose up and went out, and departed into a desert place, and there
prayed."[13]

3.

It has been the testimony of the Christian Church from
the beginning, and of the millions who "out of weakness
were made strong," that "power belongeth unto God" and
unto him alone; that his grace suffices; that "he giveth
power to the faint; and to them that have no might he
increaseth strength."[14]

What, I ask, would a man look like whom an angry
mob had stoned and finally left for dead? I knew in a
measure when I saw in an European gallery a drawing by
Rembrandt of the apostle Paul after the stoning outside the
walls of Lystra. The body lay crumpled on the ground with
the great stones scattered around it. Yet, according to Luke's
narrative, the man I saw lying there, stood up after the
stoning and walked—not away from, but back into the city
where the men lived who had stoned him, to continue
thence his work of missionary evangelization.[15] Is it a
wonder that that man later prayed that his Ephesian con-
verts might know—

"the exceeding greatness of his power to us-ward who believe, according to that working of the strength of his might which he wrought in Christ, when he raised him from the dead, and made him to sit at his right hand in the heavenly places, far above all rule, and authority, and power"?[16]

Witter, of Assam, to whom I have already alluded, a tenderly affectionate man, was furloughed home from Assam with a wife dying from cancer. Worn with the sight of her sufferings, his mind, he said, had become like a thing of wood, when an invitation came to teach a class on missions at a summer conference. Scarcely able to think, yet regarding it as God's call, he withdrew first into a quiet home in the country for a few days with the hope of pulling himself together. "I was as one in a dream," he said. "I did not see the pictures on the wall, nor the faces of the people. But before going to bed, I opened my Bible, and my eyes fell on these words: 'Seek the Lord and his strength: seek his face evermore.'[17] I told the Lord." he continued, "that I had no strength to seek his strength; but that if I had a particle of strength left, I did seek it then and there. In the night I woke up. Everything was changed. Everything seemed glorified. I looked out of the window—the face of Nature was glorified. I opened the Bible—it was glorified. I was not excited—I simply thanked God and crept into bed again. When I awoke everything was different. Now I saw the pictures on the wall. Now I saw the faces of the people. I went to the Conference, conducted the class to my satisfaction, and returning home, was able to stand by Mary's bedside and see her suffer without being moved."

Years ago in the good old "horse-and-buggy days," Dr. Somerville was jogging along a country road with Hudson

Taylor, founder of the China Inland Mission, and was commenting on the satisfaction Mr. Taylor must feel in having been personally selected by God to inaugurate that vast work for China. Mr. Taylor brushed the thought aside like a temptation, and replied, "It has often seemed to me as though God looked the whole world over to find a man who was weak enough to do his work; and when at last he found me, he said, 'He is weak enough—he will do.'"

From a purely natural point of view, I suppose that I should never have been a clergyman. Serious illness in my boyhood had left me with ravaged nerves, so that as I grew up, I saw every task through a film of fear, and dreaded every public task as though I were marching to the slaughter. Often, lying exhausted on my bed after a morning service and unable even to contemplate a service for the evening of that day, I have begun to run through the promises of God to repair the vanished strength of those who seek him:

"They that wait on the Lord shall renew their strength; they shall mount up with wings as eagles; they shall run and not be weary; and they shall walk and not faint."[18]

"So hath he [the Father] given to the Son to have life in himself; even so the Son quickeneth whom he will."[19]

"My grace is sufficient for thee: for my power is made perfect in weakness."[20]

"As the living Father sent me, and I live because of the Father; so he that eateth me, he also shall live because of me."[21]

"Wait on the Lord: and he shall strengthen thine heart."[22]

Repeating these and other like words, I have soon found myself saying, "I can do all things in him that strengtheneth me."[23] My weariness has vanished. The thing promised has passed into me. I have stood up, met my appointment, and ended the day with wonder, thanksgiving and praise.

Inspired, then, by the example of Christ, let every Christian sign forthwith his Declaration of Dependence. The Declaration of Independence we need not sign or concern ourselves with—it was signed by the forefathers long ago, and reposes safe in our country's archives. Honored by other lands, venerated by every true American, the blessings of liberty which it proclaims belong inalienably to us and to our children and will belong, we trust, to the whole world. But a Declaration *of Dependence* waits to be signed by all who stand as responsible human beings before life's inexorable demands. Supreme choices cannot be wisely made, nor can crushing burdens be victoriously borne, in disregard of the wisdom which is given without upbraiding and the power which is made perfect in weakness. He who said, "The Son can do nothing of himself,"[24] says to us, "Without me ye can do nothing."[25] God alone "hath life in himself."[26] "God hath spoken once; twice have I heard this; that power belongeth unto God."[27]

Prayer and the Needs of Others:
The Prayer of Intercession

"Father, I thank thee that thou heardest me. And I knew that thou hearest me always."

John 11:41-42 (A. R. V.)

"Simon, Simon, behold, Satan asked to have you, that he might sift you as wheat: but I made supplication for thee, that thy faith fail not."

Luke 22:31-32 (A. R. V.)

"Father, forgive them; for they know not what they do."

Luke 23:34

"Father, I desire that they also whom thou hast given me be with me where I am, that they may behold my glory."

John 17:24 (A. R. V.)

4

If prayer is heaven's gift and earth's inestimable treasure, for whom should we pray? Both for ourselves and for others? And if so, in what proportion?

For whom did Jesus pray? We have seen Jesus spending a whole night in prayer. We have seen him rise a great while before day to pray. Who on these occasions were the beneficiaries of this most costly form of spiritual exercise?

That Jesus prayed unselfishly when he prayed we might gather from the whole tenor of his life without consulting the Memoirs. His life was a river of unselfishness fed at a heavenly fountain, and sweeping all his energies into the current. See Jesus as he sits at Jacob's well in Samaria, wearied from journey, yet summoning all his powers to win to a better life a moral outcast who comes to draw water. Hear him say to the Twelve who return from the city and press him vainly to take food:

"I have meat to eat that ye know not of. My meat is to do the will of him that sent me, and to finish his work."[1]

One day Jesus' relatives and friends feared for his sanity, so lavishly did he pour out his love and power on a multitude that crowded into the house and would not so much as allow him to eat.[2] But if Jesus lived unselfishly, he prayed unselfishly, for prayer is always the index of the life, and out of the abundance of the heart the man prayeth.

An evangelist of repute is reported to have said that for two whole years he never prayed once for himself. Was he intimating that prayer for one's self is always selfish and wrong? If so, he erred. Paul the apostle prayed that his "thorn in the flesh,"[3] which he feared imperiled his efficiency as Christ's ambassador, might be removed. He also asked others to pray for him that utterance might be given him, that he might preach the Gospel boldly, as he ought to preach.

Jesus prayed for himself:

"Father, . . . glorify thy Son, that the Son may glorify thee."[4]

What is one's ultimate objective? That is the only question. If I am faced toward God's honor and the good of men, I may pray with equal freedom for myself or for others, for things great or small, material or spiritual, temporal or eternal.

That the advantage of others completely filled Jesus' horizon when he prayed is as impossible to doubt as that in the diameter and sweep of this generosity he is our perfect example. Several instances of Jesus' intercessory praying meet us in the Gospel narratives, and of these I select four: his prayer for Lazarus, his prayer for Peter, his prayer for the soldiers who crucified him, and his prayer for the Christian Church as a whole.

1.

Lazarus, though not one of the Twelve, was one of Jesus' intimate friends. With his two sisters, Mary and Martha, Lazarus played his part in making their home in Bethany, a few miles out of Jerusalem, the place of rest and consolation to which Jesus gladly turned from the strife and burden of his public ministry. There they ministered to his wants, sympathized with his sorrows, and became in turn the favored recipients of his gratitude, love and care.

So it is not surprising that when, toward the end of our Lord's ministry, Lazarus fell victim to a fatal disease, and Jesus and his disciples were across the Jordan in Perea, the call of the sisters to hasten to Lazarus' bedside was little short of a summons; and great was their dismay when, in place of responding, Jesus stayed for two whole days where he was.

But a nobler purpose than the sisters knew was maturing; and when the two days were past, Jesus said to the Twelve, "Let us go into Judea again."

"What!" they exclaimed, "back there where they were just trying to stone you?"

Assuring them that he had heaven's light on his way, Jesus said, "Our friend Lazarus is fallen asleep; but I go, that I may awake him out of sleep;" and when they again misunderstood, supposing that since the patient slept, the crisis was past and he would recover, Jesus told them plainly, "Lazarus is dead."

The meeting of Jesus with the sisters is full of pathos. Martha came first, and mingled reproach with her sorrow: "Lord, if thou hadst been here, my brother had not died." His answer was the words to which we pin our faith at every burial service:

"I am the resurrection, and the life: he that believeth on me, though he die, yet shall he live; and whosoever liveth and believeth on me shall never die."[5]

Then Mary came and fell at his feet weeping, repeating the same complaint. But now we see Jesus subject to deep emotion which vents itself in tears. "Where have ye laid him?" They went with the crowd to the tomb. Martha protested the removal of the stone: "He hath been dead four days." "Said I not unto thee," came the answer, "that if thou believedst, thou shouldest see the glory of God?" Then the stone was removed, and Jesus prayed:

"Father, I thank thee that thou heardest me. And I knew that thou hearest me always; but because of the multitude that standeth around I said it, that they may believe that thou didst send me."[6]

Having so prayed, he cried with a loud voice, "Lazarus, come forth"; and he that was dead came forth, bound hand and foot with graveclothes. "Loose him," Jesus directed, "and let him go."

Three facts of the first importance meet us in this narrative. First, Martha was right. He whom she called the Christ, the Son of God, had in his closed hand the keys of death and of the unseen world, and "even now" could recall to life Lazarus, her brother.

But Martha was also wrong. The prayer to which Lazarus was to owe his return to life was not a prayer still to be offered, like the prayer at the tomb, but a prayer that had been offered already. No further prayer was needed for Lazarus. The prayer at the tomb was not such a prayer. It was a Prayer of Thanksgiving, not of Petition. It pointed back, however, to an earlier prayer offered when Lazarus' need came first into view: "Father," Jesus prayed, "I thank thee that thou heardest me"—heardest, not hearest—"heardest me back there when, foreseeing Lazarus' sickness and death, I prayed for him, and prayed victoriously." For Jesus had not done as we might have done in his place—postponed praying till he stood with the mourners facing Lazarus' tomb. He prayed when the occasion for prayer presented itself, and prayed prevailingly.

A third fact in the narrative, quite as important, is the

fact that when Jesus prayed for Lazarus, he came into a realization of being heard. His prayer points to this:

"Father, I thank thee that thou heardest me. And I knew that thou hearest me always. . . ."

Not know now—knew then, as he prayed. Jesus prayed through. He prayed till he needed to pray no longer. He prayed until he could pray no longer because he knew that his prayer had been heard. So, as he stands at the tomb, no petition rises to his lips—only thanksgiving for what God has done and will do. He points back to the prayer already offered, not to repeat it, but to insure that those who stand by may not miss the full meaning of the august thing about to happen, when he commands the dead and the dead comes forth.

I find it quite impossible to express to others what it meant to me when I first made the discovery that I could pray till I was heard; when I realized for the first time that prayer is the arena on which faith is won; when I saw that I could pray till every fear was vanquished, every doubt dissolved, and I knew with a certitude which I could neither explain nor remove, that God had undertaken for me in the thing I desired of him. It brought heaven close to earth. It seemed a gift of grace second only to the blissful realization that God had for Christ's sake forgiven my sins.

And is not this what Jesus meant when, standing beside the fig tree withered from its roots, he said to his disciples,

"Have faith in God. Verily I say unto you, Whosoever shall say unto this mountain, Be thou taken up and cast into the sea; and shall not doubt in his heart, but shall believe that what he saith cometh to pass; he shall have it. Therefore I say unto you, All things whatsoever ye pray and ask for, *believe that ye have received them,** and ye shall have them."[1]

In the first World War I used to say this to the soldiers when they went out at night to stand guard. Never were there lonelier men or men hungrier for spiritual help. "Tell out into the sky your fears," I said, "your unsatisfied desires, your disillusionments, your shame, your heart's longings. Empty it all, as the two despondent disciples did on the way to Emmaus, into the great capacious heart of Christ. If you will set yourself to do this, and continue at it, persisting steadfastly in it, something new and wonderful will happen within you. All of a sudden you will discover that you need pray no longer. A great peace will have descended on you from heaven, and you will know that your prayer has been heard."

"But I have no faith," some may still say.

No faith, I answer, because no importunate, persistent prayer; and no importunate, persistent prayer because no controlling and commanding depth of interest. Faith is God's personal gift to those whose souls are fundamentally enlisted—who "ask, seek, knock," all three. *We must pray until we believe.*

Often when we begin, we have at best only a general faith that God is and answers prayer. As yet we have no specific faith that he will hear in the particular thing which we desire from him. But praying on, and praying through, if so be that we belong to God, we come to find that our hearts are under the sway of his Spirit, and a specific faith is added to our general faith as a gift from above; and then we find that we need not—indeed, we cannot ask

---

*The italics are mine. Right rendering of Greek aorist. American Revision margin, "received."

longer, because "we know that we have the petitions which we have asked of him."[8]

2.

Peter is by far the most fascinating and appealing of the disciples of Jesus. He was so big and warm, so tempestuous, so self-sufficient and despotic, so frail and repentant, so brim-full of encouragement for all who are in any wise like him.

More than once in the past, as I have been brooding over the lives of others and over my own, I have distinctly sensed something momentous coming—a surprise, a crisis portentous with change. Jesus foresaw such a crisis approaching in the life of Peter. A humiliation was on its way that would shatter his pride, lay his limitations nakedly bare, and bring to birth in Peter the humility which the ancient Chrysostom called "the mother of virtues."

What that humiliation was we know, and in what contrast it stood to Peter's asseverations of loyalty. It was Peter's threefold denial, at a time when Jesus was forsaken by all and on trial for his life, that he had ever known Jesus. Truly, Peter's was a fall from the heights to the depths. How a man so volatile and impetuous ever escaped the fate of Judas who, scourged by conscience, sought out a tree and hanged himself, is a mystery of grace which only Christ's intercessions for Peter seem adequate to solve.

"Simon, Simon [Jesus used Peter's weak, human name: he is not the man of rock but the man of shifting sand] behold, Satan hath desired to have you, that he may sift you as wheat: But I have prayed for thee, that thy faith fail not: and when thou art converted, strengthen thy brethren."[9]

Here once again Jesus points not to prayer in prospect but to prayer already offered. Back somewhere in the past, when Peter's constitutional frailty first came perilously into view, Jesus prayed for him—prayed, and knew as he prayed that he was heard. Jesus prayed into certitude of perfect victory for Peter, so that now, foreseeing his fall, he can hold out to Peter in advance God's certain gift of restoration to faith and a ministry on behalf of others.

3.

Crucifixion was the most hideous of deaths. It was never inflicted on a Roman. It was reserved for brigands, felons, men guilty of the most atrocious crimes. No Jew ever inflicted it. Our Lord was handed over to the Romans—given over to the wicked, men would have said in that day—to receive at their hands the detestable means of his death.

But we have glorified the Cross. We hang it in gold around our necks. We set it to flash in the sunlight on the steeples of our churches. The glory of Christ's personal triumph is so great as to have effectually banished the gloom, and we try in vain to enter into the horror that enveloped our Lord's kinsmen and disciples on that fearful morning, or that filled our Lord's own heart on the day faith now gratefully calls "Good Friday."

Strange, that order of nuns in France who practiced crucifixion as self-torture, for its process is something one cannot endure to describe. The nailing to the Cross! It was in such moments that our Lord's lips were opened, and the prayer was uttered,

"Father, forgive them; for they know not what they do."[10]

And truly, they knew not. Those men were not even real Roman soldiers. They were mercenaries, pressed into the Roman service, the offscouring of the earth, accustomed from infancy to scenes of barbarism and crime, fit instruments for such deeds as crucifixion. "Father, forgive them!" How fit the Prayer of Mercy seems for those wretched men, who stand in such contrast to those other men in priestly white whose deed the crucifixion really was. Pity, only pity in anguish fills the heart of Christ for the most depraved of men. How real his grace is! How it overleaps barriers, blots out respect of persons, and lights on the neediest of all! And can we doubt that this prayer of Christ's was heard?

> "He breaks the power of reigning sin,
>   He sets the prisoner free;
> His blood can make the vilest clean;
>   His blood availed for me."

4.

By "the Lord's Prayer" is commonly meant that brief, familiar outline of the proper objects of prayer which Jesus gave his disciples at their request, and which we habitually repeat in concert. But another prayer competes for that title—the high-priestly prayer which Jesus offered shortly before he died. The seventeenth chapter of John's Gospel is that prayer. As it sheds light on our Lord's intercessory praying, I point to three of its petitions:

There is a prayer for oneness of spirit as the perfection of love and the nerve of all persuasive testimony:

"Holy Father, keep them in thy name which thou hast given me, that they may be one, even as we are; . . . that the world may believe that thou didst send me."[11]

Divine wisdom and longing converge in this petition that rises to our Savior's lips as he commits his flock, so soon to be left defenseless in a world of ravening wolves, to his Father's care. He would that all that these fallible men ever think, will, plan, imagine or do may be securely "rooted and grounded in love." He asks the Father to guard them from every insidious threat from within—from envy, jealousy, variance, rancour, faction, strife—from all that could despoil and hurl down to hell this divinest of spiritual relationships, this sole hope of the world.

He prays also for their deliverance from all assaults of evil from without:

"I pray not that thou shouldest take them from the world, but that thou shouldest keep them from the evil one."[12]

The threat now is not from evil in the abstract, or from congenital frailty common to all the sons of Adam, or from those mass-obsessions of ignorance and madness that can sweep a world to ruin, but from "the Prince of this world"— that roaring and devouring lion, that slanderer and deceiver of the brethren, that enemy who sows tares among the wheat, robes himself as an angel of light, plots the downfall of a chief apostle, seduces the traitor, and can at last destroy both soul and body in hell.

Last of all, Jesus prays for conscious reunion with his followers in a life beyond the grave:

"Father, I desire that they also whom thou hast given me be with me where I am, that they may behold my glory, which thou hast given me: for thou lovedest me before the foundation of the world."[13]

Jesus' prayer, as he surveys the boundless future, embraces not only those who have continued with him in the temptations of his earthly life, but all who shall thereafter believe on him through their word, acknowledge him as Lord, and be gathered into the fellowship and safety of his church. What does it not mean to us, who in these latter days have believed, to know that Jesus once prayed that we too might at last be lodged safe with him in the heavenly home; and what should it not mean that his prayer on our behalf was heard? Truly—

"Every man that hath this hope in him purifieth himself, even as he is pure."[14]

* * *

Such are the Master's intercessory prayers. They point in humbling fashion to the main defect of much of our own praying—its meagre diameter and stark self-centeredness. Can over-balanced preoccupation with personal burdens, sorrows, needs and wishes ever merit the sacred name of Prayer?

One day at the prayer-hour in a seminary where I was teaching a letter was read from a young girl who was on the verge of renouncing prayer. "I never had a prayer answered," she complained. One sensed in the letter petulance and willfulness, forgiveable enough in the light of her confession—"No doubt it was all my fault." The significant thing, however, read between the lines, was the idea of prayer that had lodged itself in that girl's mind—of prayer as a convenient, supernatural way of advancing and gratifying her personal interests and desires. She coveted this, she longed for that. She asked, and there was no answer. But I cannot make God the accomplice of my own selfishness. To ask that is to number him with the transgressors in a way fatal to my own interests and the interests of others. Prayer is the privilege of those who have set out in faith to learn, admire and further the glorious purposes of a Higher Will. Only those who would weave their lives into the Kingdom's many-colored fabric may ask confidently of God. And they dare ask also for themselves, for to feed Paul is to advance Europe's evangelization, and to protect the Father's Son is to save an offering for the atoning Cross.

Let the level of prayer, then, be lifted by all who would become apt pupils in the school of Christ; and for this I suggest six alluring reasons.

1. *Prayer for others is nobly unselfish.*

Intercession is perhaps as disinterested, ardent and god-like an act as any of which our humanity is capable. Rewards obtrude too often where more conspicuous types of service are engaged in. Do I make a Christmas gift? Next year, a gift finds its way with phenomenal skill in my direction. Kindnesses are reciprocated and unselfish deeds compensated, and it is not impossible for the chance of this to steal into the field of vision and stain the unselfishness of one's thought. But this is not the case where I pray for another.

Blessings sent from heaven do not come tabbed. No television reveals to the person benefitted the face of the benefactor. He may not even know he has been prayed for. Perhaps not till both stand together in God's presence and the map of all things is spread out before their eyes will the gift of health, counsel, comfort or salvation be traced straight to the interceding plea, and intercessor and friend interceded for be linked to each other with a new bond of wonder and gratitude.

J. Campbell White, when in China, made the acquaintance of Pastor Ting Li-Mei, known as the "Moody of

China," and was shown a book in which this remarkable Christian had entered the names of some three thousand persons for whom he habitually prayed. To Dr. White's astonishment, he found his own name among them. For it had come to Pastor Ting's attention that there was an influential Christian in America by that name, and down the name went upon the list as one of the many to be prayed for. Only an accident revealed this. How many others were named in that book who will never know till the last great day the source and reason for their blessings!

2. *This is a fit and beautiful way of acknowledging the benefits we ourselves owe to the intercessions of others.*

When as a boy of twelve, smitten with scarlet fever, my life was barely saved, was it not due to the pleadings of my mother, who as nurse and intercessor, poured out her life almost unto death for me? When, grown to manhood, I once escaped being swept off my feet by fierce temptation just because I was too blind at the moment to see it, was it not because my godly father had daily prayed God to guard his son, keep him pure, and save him whole for the Christian ministry?

My parents' prayers were in front of, behind, underneath and around everything I ever thought, did or endured; and often I used to wonder what would befall me when I was deprived by death of the blessing of their prayers. Once, called to my mother's bedside, I found her in a coma and apparently near her end. As I stood there, I ventured to ask, "Mother, if you should go to heaven before I do, could you help me from there?" She roused herself back into consciousness and with the utmost decision answered, "It would not be necessary." That comforted me, for it showed that if she were taken, God could provide other praying people and I should not be bereft. He has. I never embark on any important service without the help of a score of friends who know and love the well-worn path to God's throne; and I should be ashamed if, having received what is best in life through the prayers of others, I should myself falter in this divine art and privilege of intercession.

Charles G. Finney, that great evangelist of two generations ago, was once told by those who heard him praying in a barn, "You'll kill yourself if you go on praying like that." No criticism of Mr. Finney's praying rises in my heart, for under his powerful preaching my grandfather, and a generation later my father, were converted; and may it not be that in that godly man's agonizing intercessions is to be found the reason why I am writing about prayer on behalf of others today?

3. *Praying for others is also highly advantageous to the person praying.*

It is tonic for mind and body. Why take vitamins and neglect prayer? Suppose I intercede for the Generalissimo and his tremendous Christian task for China, or for Stalin in Russia, that God will control him as he controlled Cyrus of old, or, if like Pharaoh he will not yield, make of him a blackboard on which will be written a lesson of warning for all future rulers: I cannot do this with faith and ardor without finding my mind coated with a sort of mucilage which attracts and holds for future reflection all manner of data about Russia or China, read or heard—without discovering that prayer expands the soul to the exact limit of the things prayed for. Large interests make a large nature. There are people who never have travelled but who are as large as the world.

But prayer for others means tonic also for the body. I used to suffer from insomnia. Sleepless hours ate into patience and endurance like a canker till I learned of this cure. Let the sleepless one, when he awakes, put a shawl over his shoulders and a pillow behind his back, and then let him ask himself two questions: First, what law of life have I been violating? If none, then who is it that God has awakened me to pray for? Let him pray for this one, for that one, and for a score more whose needs are as great or greater than his own. Then let him lay his head upon his pillow, and if his experience is like mine, restlessness and worry will have vanished, and he can say—

"He giveth his beloved sleep."[15]

"In peace will I both lay me down and sleep; For thou, Jehovah, alone makest me dwell in safety."[16]

4. *Prayer for others is mighty in influence—perhaps the most strategic use of time and strength open to mortals.*

Dr. McCune, once missionary in Korea, awoke one night concerned for George, a Korean convert. His wife tried to quiet him: "You are over-strained and nervous." "No, I see George, and he is in trouble," was his reply. "I must get up and pray for him." When George told the story of that night, how he had been captured and put to torture, saying *"and then Jesus came, and it was all right,"* then Dr. McCune knew that his intercessory prayer that night had been both inspired and honored.

In London, years ago, I was told that I must on no account leave the city without hearing Archdeacon Basil Wilberforce. The fame of that name in the story of British philanthrophy persuaded me, and I arrived at St. John's Chapel to find it crowded to the doors. The Archdeacon, in a scarlet robe, aged, pallid, almost transparently thin, stood before us, bringing to the attention of the congregation cases of need for united intercession. A case would be mentioned, and then a silence would follow in which all prayed. I recall the Archdeacon's words as he brought for our prayer a poor sick girl in the East End of London: "Now let us ask God," he said, "to send down a whole bevy of bright angels to her bedside." Silence followed as we prayed, and need I add that as I left the Chapel, my feet seemed hardly to touch the ground?

5. *Prayer for other people is like a bright door through which one passes into a new acquaintance and fellowship with Christ.*

How could it be otherwise? The same Bible that tells us that two cannot walk together except they be agreed, assures us that the absorbing occupation of our exalted Lord in heaven is intercession.[17] How, then, is it possible to enter on a ministry identical with his without our paths meeting? Who, after praying for others, has not risen from his knees to find the air luminous, and the separating veil thin that hid from him the face of the Great Companion, the Heavenly Intercessor?

6. *Unselfish prayer for others is the one ministry required of all Christians.*

Paul, as he brought to a close his letter to the Colossians, left a personal message for one of its members:

"Say to Archippus, Take heed to the ministry which thou hast received in the Lord, that thou fulfil it."[18]

What Archippus' ministry was the Apostle did not disclose. It was a ministry within his powers, needed by the community, and assigned him by the Lord. Now without doubt every Christian is an Archippus, with a separate task suited to his aptitudes and definitely assigned him; but prayer on behalf of others is a ministry within the reach of all and required of all. Alas for us, and alas for others whom we might benefit, if we ignore it!

Dr. Jowett, lamented Christian preacher of fragrant memory, once remarked that he would rather teach one man to pray than ten men to preach. He said also that he never learned so much about prayer as he did one day when he overheard a woman, in agony, pour out her soul in confession of the sins of another just as though those sins were her own. There in a picture is our ministry of intercession filmed before our eyes!

It was for this, so we are told, that Christ—

"loosed us from our sins by his blood, and he made us to be a kingdom, to be priests unto his God and Father." [19]

That passage from the Revelation, containing as it does our credentials as intercessors, deserves scrutiny. The King James Version rendered it differently—

"made us to be kings and priests unto his God and Father."

That was confusing. "Kings"? Yes, we should all like to be kings and rule; but "priests" also? How unite functions so vast and different? But in the ancient book of Exodus, I found the key:

"Ye shall be unto me a kingdom of priests, and a holy nation." [20]

That clarified everything. God alone is King, and under him are his people, *all of them priests*. Authorized by divine appointment, armed with the all-conquering blood of Christ, and led by the Spirit, they are to pray down from the skies forgiveness and reconciliation upon alienated, groping and suffering humanity. They are to link earth to heaven by their intercessions and so bring in the promised kingdom of God.

May a promise left by John, the beloved disciple, hearten every follower of Christ for his appointed ministry:

"If any man see his brother sinning a sin not unto death, he shall ask, and God will give him life for them that sin not unto death."[21]

A dark shadow, it is true, falls athwart the verse. We cannot miss its allusion to that open-eyed, contemptuous rejection of all truth and goodness which Jesus during his earthly ministry called blasphemy against the Holy Spirit, and which he said should never be forgiven, whether in this world or in the world to come.[22] That human sin can go so far in despite of self-immolating divine love is a spiritual mystery before which we can only bow our heads, leaning solely on Jesus' word, and lifting a heartfelt prayer that in the last, great day that sin of sins may be laid to the charge of but few.

But brightly shines the promise of Life against the tragic possibilities of sin and death! LIFE—what is it? Is there anything greater? SPIRITUAL LIFE is a great composite. It is more than Repentance, more than Faith, more than Forgiveness. It is more than Love, Joy and Peace, and all the other fruits and spices of the Spirit. It is all that humanity longs for, all that it lost through sin, all that Christ will yet restore when redemption is complete and humanity is brought to its full salvation. God will give LIFE to those for whom we pray; and can we ever look into God's face unashamed if we fail in this ministry.

Prayer and Life's Benefits:
The Prayer of Thanksgiving

*"Jesus therefore took the loaves;
and having given thanks, he distributed to them that were set down."*

John 6:11 (A. R. V.)

*"Father, I thank thee that thou
heardest me."*

John 11:41 (A. R. V.)

*"I thank thee, O Father, Lord of
heaven and earth, that thou didst
hide these things from the wise and
understanding, and didst reveal them
unto babes."*

Luke 10:21 (A. R. V.)

*"And he received a cup, and when
he had given thanks, he said, Take
this, and divide it among yourselves."*

Luke 22:17 (A. R. V.)

5

VERY early in life I was taught to give thanks, for when we were all young children at home together, my father taught us to pray. He gave us this simple, threefold recipe: THANK, CONFESS, ASK. What good thing had happened to us last week? We were to thank God for it. What had we done that was wrong, or failed to do that was right? We were to confess it. What did we need or desire? We were to ask God for it. Who could not pray with that simple formula before him?

The order, too, was correct. Thanksgiving first—that is common politeness. When I meet a friend on the street who has done me a favor, do I talk about a dozen other things before acknowledging his kindness? No, I thank him first of all. And there is a further reason for putting thanksgiving first, for thanskgiving is an elevator that lifts me up and up till I can look out on my whole life and see it sunlit with God's greatness and goodness. Then, when I have thanked God, it is only natural to confess the faults which stand in contrast to his goodness; and when I have both thanked and confessed, I am in a mood to ask. No one is likely to pray for a mean or selfish thing who has begun his prayer with thanksgiving and confession.

But Father did still more for us. He saw to it that we prayed in this way. Every Sunday afternoon he would gather us children with Mother around him, and after a brief, practical homily touching character or behavior,

73

would have us all kneel. The youngest knelt beside him, prayed first. and had the fit word put in her mouth when she stumbled. The next in age followed, then the next, till all six of us and Mother had prayed. Last of all, Father prayed, led us in the Lord's Prayer, and the little service was over. Though he had been pastor of churches, and for over forty years president of a theological seminary, in his earlier ministry public prayer had seemed an almost insurmountable task, so in this way he sought to make less difficult to his children what to him had been a trial. In this way he has also left an object-lesson for parents with little children, in the years before the youngsters are old enough to scatter and get away with their friends Sunday afternoons.

It is no surprise to those who read their Bibles to find that the prayers of our great Exemplar abounded in thanksgiving. That followed from the perfection of his vision and the spontaneity of his nature. We mortals feel our way into the future. After putting into requisition every glint of light available to us—conscientious thought, scanning the Scriptures, counsel with others, and prayer —we can at best say, "This seems to be God's will for me." We grope our way—Jesus saw his. He walked in bright sunlight. He saw God's finger pointing the way.

"The Son can do nothing of himself but what he seeth the Father doing: for what things soever he doeth, these the Son also doeth in like manner."[1]

No wonder the areas of God's providential control widened before his eyes till they became co-extensive with life itself, and seeing his Father everywhere and rejoicing in him, Jesus became the consummate exposition of Paul's rule of life,

"In everything give thanks, for this is the will of God in Christ Jesus concerning you."[2]

Jesus' thanksgivings illustrate the joyous side of prayer. We are prone to forget that although he was "a man of sorrows, and acquainted with grief," his was also the most radiant joy ever felt. Jesus dwelt beside the twin-fountains of joy—perfection of fellowship and perfection of obedience, and we find his joy overflowing in four recorded Prayers of Thanksgiving: (1) when he fed five thousand hungry people; (2) when he praised God for answered prayer at Lazarus' grave; (3) when seventy of his followers returned from a tour of evangelization with shouts of victory; and (4) when at the Last Supper he took bread and wine, tragic symbols of his sacrificial death, and thanked God for them.

1.

Jesus was on the farther side of the Galilean lake where thousands of people had assembled to see and hear him. Far from home, many of them had become faint for lack of food; and Jesus disposed them in companies upon the grass and organized his disciples as waiters to serve them. Then he took five little barley-loaves—not unlike our small buns —and two small fish, "said grace," and proceeded to distribute what to the wonder of beholders became more than a sufficiency for all. The enthusiasm of the crowd may easily be imagined.

A very good man, office-bearer in a church of mine, told me one day that he had discontinued the practice of grace before meals in his home because in the hurry of the day the truths symbolized tended to become dim and the form of words mechanical and insincere. Five minutes of medita-

tion in advance would of course have made the spiritual
fact resplendent with present meaning, but such preparation the speed of his life did not allow. But when Jesus
took the loaves that day and gave thanks for them, his
words were not without their full content of meaning.
The creative power and providential care of God were too
vividly present for that.

To begin with, there was the lad who had got started
round the head of the lake at the right time with the
adults, and had come safe and sound to the place where
Jesus and his disciples were. Next, there was the mother,
who had supplied him with a tiny lunch to keep him satisfied and contented while away. Third, there was Andrew's
contact with that highly useful child. Fourth, and more
remarkable, there was the lad's readiness to surrender his
lunch to a stranger for a purpose he could neither foresee
nor comprehend. Last of all, and even more mysterious,
there was the boundless, brooding, creative power of God,
choosing

"the weak things of the world, . . . to put to shame the things that
are strong; . . . and the things that are not, that he might bring
to nought the things that are: that no flesh should glory before God."[8]

Now if all of these five indispensable links of the providential chain are manifest to my mind in its dullness,
what wealth of spiritual fact and truth may not have been
manifest to the mind of Jesus, who saw not only intricate
providential preparations and fragments of food multiplied
to the advantage of fainting thousands, on that day many
centuries ago, but also, thrown on the screen of future
history, an incomparable picture of himself as the Bread
of Life, broken and distributed for the redemption of the
world!

2.

Having already considered Jesus' Prayer of Thanksgiving at Lazarus' tomb, I need not return to it, unless to point to a divine paradox—the juxtaposition there of grief and joy in a perfect being, the intermingling of the divine and the human in the soul of the Son of man.

For both grief and joy ruled alternately in the heart of Jesus that day. Joy was there, deep and strong, in sure expectation of prayer's answer. Sleeping Lazarus was to be awakened. The Son's relationship to the Father was to be certified. Fountains of consolation were to be opened for grieving humanity never to run dry till the resurrection morn.

Many, very many since that day have known Jesus' joy of answered prayer. He had promised it to his followers:

"Hitherto have ye asked nothing in my name: ask, and ye shall receive, that your joy may be perfect" (*parfait*, French translation) .ᵃ

Once at the close of a religious service a young woman asked me, "Do you recall speaking about Prayer in such and such a church one Sunday? I was in despair that day," she continued, "and ready to abandon my Christian faith as an insincere and useless thing. But I took heart, and prayed again; and I want you to know that I have had my first experience of answered prayer!" And what a light overspread her face as she said it!

Yet it was at the grave of Lazarus that this joy of Jesus was drenched in tears, for it is there that we come upon that shortest and saddest verse in the Bible, "Jesus wept." Even the prospect of the joy about to break on the heads of the mourners failed to block the path of Jesus' grief or turn his tears into surface tears, for on the testimony of the beloved evangelist, the grief of Jesus was paroxysmal.

Yet I see celestial light shining through the tears of Jesus. For what does it mean that Jesus weeps and groans aloud even when help is near—that he is himself as mightily shaken as are Martha and Mary even when the power of Lazarus' resurrection is safely clasped in his shut hand? It means that heaven *grieves at our grief;* weeps with us when we have no cause or justification for our weeping; weeps when, in but a trifling moment, all ground for sorrow will be past and the tears and wails of the mourners replaced with the tumultuous joy of resurrection!

3.

It should be an encouraging fact to every earnest Christian that thanksgiving in the life of Jesus reached its acme when men chosen to be his fellow-warriors in the battle against evil proved successful in their mission and returned with victory perching on their banners. This took place when seventy of Jesus' disciples returned from an evangelistic mission all aglow with the tidings that even the demons had been subject to them through appeal to the authority of Jesus' name.

It was the last effort at general evangelization before Jesus suffered. Never had there been so many dispatched. Since two banded in fellowship are more than twice one, they were sent out in pairs, and with explicit instructions. There were to be no packed suitcases, no expense-funds, no palavering on the road, no restlessness over discomforts, no resentment where hospitality was denied. When met with a cold stare and told to move on they were to breathe only benedictions of peace. They would come away none the poorer—their peace would come rebounding in blessing on their heads. When finally driven forth, they were to wipe the dust of the unbelieving place from their sandals in symbolic appeal, testifying that the long-expected kingdom of God had once drawn near and had forever departed.

The victory of the Seventy was complete, yet no surprise to the Master. While they had been working he had been praying. Before the feeble word of these "babes" the foundations of the underworld had begun to crumble —"I beheld Satan as lightning fall from heaven," he told them. Yet let them not be unduly exultant but rejoice with trembling. Peril lurked in an experience of the divine power. God's presence in a human soul was the chief thing, and far more than any of its manifestations.

"Rejoice not, that the spirits are subject unto you; but rather rejoice, because your names are written in heaven."[5]

Charles G. Finney, the great evangelist—so my father, who once lived in his home, used to tell me—after a service in which many had been converted and the power of God had been conspicuously manifested, would return home, throw himself face-downward on the floor of his room, and remain prone until he was set free from the perilous illusion that it was his own gifts and powers, and not God's, that had wrought the transformations he had witnessed. Not until his spirit was prostrate before God in humility could the work of the Spirit, he knew, go on.

Now against this background of victory the joy of Jesus burst forth unconfined. More majestic than the stilling of the sea, more wonderful than the raising of Lazarus, was the might that had used these frail followers of a despised

Messiah to blast the very foundations of Satan's rule. A radiance distinguished the gladness of Jesus that pointed straight to its heavenly source—Luke has captured it in the phrase, joy "in the Holy Spirit." It was the gladness Peter has called "joy unspeakable and full of glory," and we may best approach it through the channel of the written word:

"I thank thee, O Father, Lord of heaven and earth, that thou hast hid these things from the wise and prudent, and hast revealed them unto babes: even so, Father; for so it seemed good in thy sight."[6]

Who are the "wise and prudent"? The wise in their own eyes, of course; the self-satisfied and self-sufficient who, knowing already, or possessed of power to know, can be taught by neither God nor man. The "babes"— who are they? The docile, the "poor in spirit," the aspiring, who, knowing nothing as they ought to know, are wide-open to light and leading from above. Jesus looks on these invincible disseminators of the true wisdom and rejoices. Who but his Father would ever have elected men disdained for their scholastic incompetence, to tear down man's fallacious thinking and rear the august structure of truth in its place? "Not many wise are called." God has written it into the very fabric of the universe that the proud and self-satisfied man shall never know. Jesus thanks God for this. It is right that it should be so.

So there emerge wonder and thanksgiving for the function of revelation which is solely his as the Father's Son:

"All things are delivered unto me of my Father: and no man knoweth who the Son is, but the Father; and who the Father is, but the Son, and he to whom the Son will reveal him."[7]

Jesus is the Great Incommensurable, the Super-eminent Mystery, the Sole Repository. Everything the Seventy possessed or imparted was first in him as personal faith and achievement. The mystery of his own being Jesus can neither impart nor hide from his disciples. It is the Father's secret, though in the faith he inspires and the authority he delegates they begin to discern it. As Tennyson once quoted, when asked to "classify" Christ: "No man knoweth the Son, but the Father."

Weightier still in Jesus' thought, however, is the distinction bestowed on him as sole revealer of the Father. To the unrenewed mind of man, the Father remains ever an impenetrable secret till the Son makes him known.

"No man cometh unto the Father but by me."[8]

"He that hath seen me hath seen the Father."[9]

Doctrine this? Not so. Experience. Far-away discernment of God as a cosmic fact, inferred from or revealed in phenomena, may be open to any rational mind, but not the knowledge that enraptures and transforms. That is Jesus' gift. He not only reveals—*he manifests*. He enters the human heart and brings the Father with him.

How far we, the intelligentsia, have drifted from this! We would make a God out of concepts much as our cook makes a batch of muffins. We toss unity, infinity and causality into the theological bowl; next, intelligence, benevolence and will; then omniscience, omnipotence and omnipresence. Then we add a scant half-dozen ethical attributes and a generous dash of personality, give the whole thing a tremendous intellectual beating, and turn out—what? Nothing that will rise, brown, or do anything but mess up the theological kitchen. Wherein are we better, Isaiah asks us, than his idolaters with "a tree that will not rot," their gold, silver and "cunning workman"?[10]

A youngster of ten in a Cleveland church was asked recently why Jesus ever came to earth, and this was his answer: "People wanted to see God. Now God is spirit, and you can't see a spirit. So Jesus came, lived and taught. But people still wanted to see God. So Jesus said to them, 'You want to see God, do you? Well, *just look at me!*'" Once more "out of the mouths of babes and sucklings"! Father, Lord of heaven and earth, I thank thee!

4.

A fourth Prayer of Thanksgiving is recorded in Jesus' Memoirs. It was offered at the Last Supper, when Jesus took the cup which was filled with bitterness for him but has been filled to overflowing with joy, peace and salvation for us, and thanked God for it. As this prayer seems in substance more closely joined with the Prayer of Submission, its treatment may best be left to the next chapter.

5.

How much there is to thank God for even with our world in a tumult of doubt and agony. We admit that the clouds never looked blacker, yet the Star of Truth never shone more brightly over our heads than now. The conviction never burned more brightly that truth is better than illusion and knowledge than error for a race with a future. The prewar veneer that hid greed, rage and hate behind a smiling exterior deceives us no longer. More bandages have been torn from human eyes than ever before. More people see the sin of selfishness and the selfishness of sin. More recognize the inhumanity of our finance, the tawdriness of our culture, the godlessness of our education, the suicidal quality of our international relations and the hopelessness of our atheism and unbelief. More are ready at last to hear the word which the Lord Christ is speaking to all dictators, kings, presidents, mayors, judges, college presidents and big-business men today: "Every plant which my heavenly Father hath not planted shall be rooted up."[11] The rooting-up is on now. We are in the throes of world-revolution. There is in the human family a spirit of treason and destructive malice which seems equal, should the hand of God not restrain, to tearing down all that the generations have builded and finally, like Samson of old, perishing itself in the ruin. We tremble at the power of selfish individualism and godless nationalism to defy and halt the good. Yet these grim facts do not obliterate the stars of Faith, Hope and Love that shine never so brightly in the heavens. Christianity has not been for nearly twenty centuries in the world to leave ideals and institutions unaffected. The leaven has been hid, but it has been operating. The yearning of humanity for peace has become almost an audible cry. Men are casting out demons and proclaiming truth on every side who give no hint of conscious union with the Christian society. Unselfish spirits are laboring by thousands in groups and alone to bind up the wounds and allay the fever of the world—tangible matters, it would seem, for thanksgiving.

Men call the Church of Christ "apostate" today, yet it has never yet repudiated the Sacred Documents which condemn its vagaries and infidelities. They are read in its services every Sunday. The poor in spirit, the meek, the merciful, the hungry for righteousness, the peacemakers—these are still the light of the world. There is scarcely a church in which the prophet's "remnant" may not be found that has never bowed the knee to any popular idol; men and women who, when cynics cry, "Who will show us any good?" and when false prophets chirp and mutter, lift holy hands to heaven in the prayer God never refused: "Lord, lift thou up the light of thy countenance upon us." They still place Intercession at the heart of the Christian enterprise. They sow the pure truth of the Word broadcast on the hearts of the accessible and susceptible. They are content to work in painful and obscure places if only the underprivileged, the "sheep without a shepherd," may be found, fed and safely folded. They dread no cataclysms, for their Lord expected them. Though the earth do change and the mountains be shaken into the heart of the seas, they will not fear. Christ is sufficient. His salvation is complete. They wonder daily at the particularity of God's providence and the safety of all who put their trust in him. They find in days when all but the heavenly things are being shaken that the star of Hope shines not less brightly but more brightly than ever before.

If the great things seem still shrouded in mystery, let us thank God for the simple things, for this is the will of God in Christ Jesus concerning us. Let us thank God for these blessings—

Bread, in the measure he gives it.

Work, if the chance is still ours, and a chance to seek it or share it with the brother who lacks it.

Friendship's cup, ever sparkling, ever full.

Human love, that bright angel sent down to smooth every rough path and brighten every dark hour.

"Home, sweet Home."

Nature, her power to thrill or calm, her thunder-peal, her mother-touch, her divine instructiveness.

Music, a language rapt as from some far-off sphere, bearing overtones like the beatings of an Immortal Heart, like the echoes of an Everlasting Sea.

Let us thank God for a new and richer opportunity to trust him, and to show by filial obedience how good and great and just and merciful we believe and know him to be. Our fathers trusted God, and he delivered them. Why should not we, their sons and daughters?

6.

At the close of a prayer service in a New York church a gentle, gray-haired man stood and said, "I have been making a list of God's mercies to me. The list is long. I have counted seventy-five of them." A week or so later, the same old man, smiling sweetly, arose and said, "My list of blessings is growing. I have now counted eighty-three of them."

David of old tried to count God's mercies and failed:

"Many, O Lord my God, are thy wonderful works which thou hast done, and thy thoughts which are to us-ward: they cannot be reckoned up in order unto thee: if I would declare and speak of them, they are more than can be numbered."[12]

David failed. But try, even if you fail. And alas, alas, for the many who have failed because they never tried!

"Whoso offereth praise glorifieth me."[13] No one can make God more glorious than he is. All can make God appear glorious, as he is, both to themselves and to others.

Prayer and the Will of God:
The Prayer of Submission

"Abba, Father, all things are possible unto thee; remove this cup from me: howbeit not what I will, but what thou wilt."

Mark 14:36 (A. R. V.)

"[Jesus] began to be greatly amazed and sore troubled. And he saith unto them, My soul is exceeding sorrowful even unto death."

Mark 14:33-34 (A. R. V.)

6

The light fades as we turn from the Prayer of Thanksgiving to the Prayer of Submission. We pass into thick shadow, and dread of menacing evil grips the heart.

Though Jesus has been wont to resort there as a place for prayer, the Garden of Gethsemane now is dark with night. It is not favoritism for Jesus to choose only Peter, James and John to be his companions: he can draw nearer to three than he can to eleven, and what these future "pillars" of the early Church gain tonight they will in due time be sharing with all. We draw near too, for a vital lesson on the art of praying waits to be taught us in the Garden.

1.

Mark's vivid narrative furnishes the few outward facts. First, he pictures the distraction and desolation of Jesus' soul:

He "began to be greatly amazed and sore troubled. And he saith unto them, My soul is exceeding sorrowful even unto death."[1]

Have you ever felt yourself on the verge of panic, and saying, "Just a little more, and I could lose self-command, and be swept into chaos?"

"Greatly amazed" means just that. "Sore troubled" adds its own touch. From the Greek, ἀδημονέω, it describes the desolation of a soul "far from home."

"Exceeding sorrowful even unto death" completes the picture.

One day during the first World War, a soldier was carried past me to the base hospital on a stretcher. "What is his trouble?" I asked.

"Homesickness," was the reply.

I never knew till then that homesickness could lay one so low.

A few strokes of Mark's pen suffice for the remaining details, Jesus—

"Fell on the ground."

One is indeed "clean-forspent" who prays like that.

A thrice-repeated supplication follows:

"Abba, Father, all things are possible unto thee; remove this cup from me: howbeit not what I will, but what thou wilt."

Then a fruitless quest for human sympathy:

"And he cometh, and findeth them sleeping, and saith unto Peter, Simon, . . . couldest thou not watch with me one hour?"

Then—this told by Luke the physician:

"And being in an agony he prayed more earnestly; and his sweat became as it were great drops of blood falling down upon the ground."[2]

Then, total transformation and deliverance! Weakness transcended! Victory won!—

"Sleep on now, and take your rest: it is enough; the hour is come; behold, the Son of man is betrayed into the hands of sinners."

It is as though Jesus said, "I have no further need of your help"; and the records attest the calm that thenceforth never forsook him as he passed to the informal examination under Annas, the trial before Caiaphas, the condemnation, the scourging, and the journey to the Cross.

2.

What now, have we here? The actual Gethsemane experience of Jesus? No, scarcely more than signposts pointing towards it. We are left where the three were left— before an unplumbed mystery, before depths too profound and too holy for us. The unseen fact, the divine accomplishment which is of the very substance of our faith, remains strange to us. Are we asleep as the disciples were? Are we too shallow, too sinful, to vibrate to the ocean-tempests of Gethsemane?

We seem surer of what Christ's agony was not than of what it was. It was not the shrinking of a sensitive soul from a cruel and painful death. If frail martyrs could face torture without flinching, did not their Lord? Green, in his *History of the English People,* tells us how powerless the terror of death was against the British martyrs. Rogers, a fellow-worker with Tyndale in the translation of the Bible and one of the foremost of the Protestant preachers, "died bathing his hands in the flame as if it had been cold water."

"Play the man, Master Ridley," cried Latimer, as at Oxford the flames shot up around him; "we shall ˙this day light such a candle, by God's grace, in England as I trust shall never be put out." Plato tells us in the *Phaedo* that Socrates, whom we often class among the pagans, "in the easiest and gentlest manner, without the least fear or change of color or feature, and looking at his gaoler with all his eyes, as his manner was, held the cup to his lips, and quite cheerfully and readily drank off the poison," while the rude gaoler who guarded him "burst into tears, turned away and went out". So our soldier boys went to

meet pain and death without shrinking, surrendering all
for the liberties of the world.

Nor could the agony of Jesus in the Garden be traced
to the shame heaped upon him, to the ignominy, or to a
sense of personal failure— "who for the joy that was set
before him endured the cross, *despising the shame.*" Nor
was its source uncertainty—the glimmering of a hope, cher-
ished in brighter days and never relinquished, that a hap-
pier issue might yet crown his ministry; that God might
interpose at the eleventh hour, as he had so often done
for ancient Israel, and grant a deliverance which was now
to be wrung from him by prayer. If our Lord's pleadings
in the Garden seem to allow this, it is as certainly dis-
allowed and excluded by the clear program of messianic
suffering with which he began his ministry, and by the
systematic course of instruction he proceeded to give his
disciples on the divine necessity of his death. For was it
not Jesus who, on the road to Emmaus a few days later,
rebuked two forlorn disciples whose faith had been con-
founded by his crucifixion, saying to them, "O foolish men,
and slow of heart to believe in all that the prophets have
spoken! Behooved it not the Christ to suffer these things,
and to enter into his glory?"[3] Had he who rebuked them
been "foolish and slow of heart to believe" just three days
before?

3.

If ever light is shed on the mystery of Gethsemane and
the Cross, it will be once more through words written for
our learning, through "all that the prophets have spoken":

"He was wounded for our transgressions, he was bruised for our
iniquities; the chastisement of our peace was upon him; and with his
stripes we are healed."[4]

"Behold the Lamb of God, which taketh away the sin of the world."[5]

"Him who knew no sin he made to be sin on our behalf; that we might become the righteousness of God in him."[6]

"We see Jesus, who was made a little lower than the angels for the suffering of death, crowned with glory and honor; that he by the grace of God should taste death for every man."[7]

Light streams from those Scriptures today. They bring a cleansing of the air and a lifting of the heart to millions whose faith, but for them, would have been submerged with Jesus in the tragedy of Gethsemane and Calvary. The "wounding," the "bruising," the "being made sin on our behalf"—fearful representation, that last, of the depths to which God's Son descended that we might be made partakers of his holiness!—what are they but the "bitter herbs"[8] of the Passover, distilled into the cup which Jesus prayed might pass from him in the Garden; which he tasted there, drained with unresisting lips on Calvary, and has now filled with joy, peace and blessing for all who accept and adore him. Jesus in the Garden "tasted death for every man." That is the key to Gethsemane.

We must revise our vocabulary if we are to take in the stature of our salvation and pray the Prayer of Submission as Jesus did. "Death" must come to mean to us what it meant to him who "tasted" it. In common parlance death means little more than the parting of a tired soul from an outworn body. Angels attend it as it slips its moorings. As a child drops asleep, so eyes close on the disillusionment, sin and sorrow of our mortality to open on the *things which eye hath not seen, nor ear heard, neither have entered into the heart of man.* What wonder that the Scriptures refuse to denominate such a translation into life

"death," and reserve the name for the banishment of incorrigible souls into the outer darkness where God is no
longer revealed and where sin has its way and works its
final will. No one who has come to understand by "death"
what Jesus tasted in Gethsemane, could ever commit
suicide.

So our thoughts begin to move on the plane on which
Jesus' thought moves:

"Our friend Lazarus is fallen asleep; but I go, that I may awake
him out of sleep."⁹

Of the daughter of Jairus, he says,

"The child is not dead, but sleepeth."¹⁰

And in this parlance of faith the Apostolic Church follows
its Lord:

"But we would not have you ignorant, brethren, concerning them
that fall asleep; that ye sorrow not, even as the rest, who have no hope.
For if we believe that Jesus died and rose again, even so them also who
have been *put to sleep by Jesus* will God bring with him."*

What has become our lot, however, was not the lot of
Jesus. He tasted what we need never taste. Joined volun-
tarily and irrevocably to a world that had forsaken God,
he found himself forsaken. The everlasting arms on which,
from the beginning, he had leaned, he felt no more. The
face of the Father who had never left him alone, he could
not find. The bitterness was the bitterness of separation.
The cry from the Cross:

"My God, my God, why hast thou forsaken me?" ¹¹

forever declares this.

*1 Thess. 4: 13-14. The passive verb with $\delta\iota\acute{a}$ and the genitive can mean
nothing else than this. The picture is that of a mother putting her tired
child to sleep. So Professor Johannes Weiss, radical theologian, pointed out
to me years ago in Marburg, before the land of Luther and Melanchthon had
specialized on war.

In a dream not long ago, I thought I heard that cry. It seemed to me the most terrible cry ever heard by mortals—the cry of divine purity and uttermost love despised, rejected and forsaken. I saw the souls of men who did not respond to that cry haled before an outraged universe and adjudged dead to all chivalry and nobility, for at last the whole world seemed to know God's answer to his Son's question, "WHY?"

In the Garden of Gethsemane Jesus prayed the Prayer of Submission. In his first plea he subordinated his will to his Father's. In his last, he abandoned his will for his Father's. Jesus chose the Father's will and way in lieu of his own, and prayed that at whatever cost it might prevail. Thus the doubting question is forever disposed of, "Was the prayer of Jesus in the Garden answered or unanswered?" As we are told plainly elsewhere, he was "heard for his godly fear."[12] In the Garden, the enemy's frowning fortress of hate and terror was blown to bits. Reared by the Prince of this world in the path of the world's Saviour, it no longer blocked his way, and the Captain of our salvation marched unopposed to his Cross to save us. Having given him up for us, the Father "spared not his own Son."[13] Having come into the world to save sinners, "himself he cannot save."[14] O faithful saying![15] O Grace abounding![16] O Love that would not let us go!

4.

How, I now ask, does Jesus' Prayer of Submission bear on the praying of those who would follow in his footsteps? How can men and women as frail as we ourselves are pray with sincerity this hardest and yet most indispensable of all prayers? First, I answer, we must gain insight into the surpassing excellence of our Father's character and will. Then, our eyes must be anointed to see the areas of God's Providence widen until they safely cover even the most tragic experiences of life.

Some will not take kindly to my title, the Prayer of Submission. To some, it will seem needlessly harsh, implying an antagonism between ourselves and God which could not exist if we lived and loved with all the ardor of the First and Great Commandment. Would not the Prayer of Acquiescence be nobler and serve equally well?

Yet the Prayer of Submission conforms better to the facts. For as our life unfolds, situations emerge in which God's plans for us fall sharply athwart our human desires and expectations, and when the contrast and opposition are clearly revealed, acquiescence in God's way is bound to involve a struggle, if not a sharp battle.

In a home I once knew, a daughter lay dead on the very eve of her marriage, the next room filled with her wedding presents. When God, who does not willingly afflict, said "No" to all their prayers and hopes, was acquiescence easy?

Few of us are destined to live out our days without coming to some crisis in which it will take all the grace heaven can give to enable us to say, "Father, thy will is, and must be, what thine Apostle, specialist in suffering, said it was—'good, and acceptable, and perfect,'[17] and better than my own in the matter; and although my heart is breaking, I bow to thy way, relinquishing my own." Wonderful it is, and strengthening, to think that in the sufferings and prayers of such hours, Jesus has gone before us to be our perfect example.

I knew a woman allotted to stand on the shore of Long

Island Sound and see her son, grown to manhood, drown before her eyes. "I threw myself on the sand," she told me afterward, "and told God that I would not rise from that place until he gave me power to smile through my tears." And God gave her her request. What made such self-conquest possible? It was because she knew personally the character, the power and the love of God.

So let us begin by confessing that the will of God to many of us is a blight, a shadow, an inscrutable and inexorable hostile power thwarting our poor human wills and blocking their way to self-realization and happiness. To some, regarded as intelligent and even as Christian, "all hope is gone," and "the will of God be done," mean the identical thing. And yet if God's will were that hostile thing, it would not only be irrational—it would be a spiritual crime to pray the Prayer of Submission.

How very different is the fact. A mother and her very young child were conferring, as mothers and children often do, on deep and heavenly things. "What does God look like?" the child asked; and without waiting, he answered himself, laboriously saying the big syllables: "I think I know—I think he looks like the be—ootiful colors in the sky, when the sun is go—ing down." "Out of the mouths of babes and sucklings" once more!

To gain a true thought of God and God's will, I must glean from memory all the beautiful and noble things I have ever felt or seen or heard—the sunsets and the rainbows; the birds and the flowers; the majestic trees; the fair-haired children dancing with glee; the purity of Alpine summits at dawn; the bubbling gladness of Mozart and the spirituality of Bach; earth's noblest deeds of heroism and sacrifice; the loyalty and affection of the dearest friends I have ever known; my mother's love; my father's prayers. All these, multiplied, magnified, fused into one, and launched with an abandon of pity for a sorrowing, sin-cursed universe, are only one tiny ray from the nobility and the glory of the will of God. God's will is the same as the will of Jesus. Indeed, Jesus was "God manifest in the flesh."

What is God's will? It is just *God willing*. If God is love,[18] then it is Infinite Love willing—planning, devising, purposing, ordaining, for the happiness and holiness of his creatures. When God's will becomes that, it is no longer impossible to pray the Prayer of Submission as Jesus did. As the thirty-seventh Psalm bids us, we can *trust in the Lord, delight ourselves in the Lord, commit our way unto the Lord, rest in the Lord.*

5.

Then, for the second step, and to make the foregoing doubly sure, the areas of God's providential care must widen before our eyes till they become conterminous with life, and we see every experience life can bring stamped with the signet ring of his permission and sheltered safe within his care.

A preacher once read to his congregation those words of Christ, "The very hairs of your heads are all numbered";[19] and then, leaning earnestly over the pulpit, he added, "Some of you do not believe that *even your heads* are numbered!" A startling charge that. Was it true? It provokes a sober question: How much am I entitled to believe about God's Providence? How much that vitally affects me may I trust it to safely include?

A man stood in a railroad station facing two trains.

bound by different routes for his destination. He chose one of them. The other, he afterwards learned, left the track, and with terrible consequences to the passengers. He came to a friend of mine, all aglow with the deliverance, exclaiming, "What a wonderful Providence!" My friend, a wiser man than he, answered simply, "What about the people on the other train?"

Well, what about them? Were they outside the areas of God's thought and care? Was there no Providence for them?

When we are young and immature, we interpret God's Providence in terms of the manifestly favorable. He gave me this. He delivered me from that. This is as necessary as it is instinctive, for it is only as we are blessed with some obvious good or rescued from some obvious evil that the idea of a higher "Watchcare" dawns on us. But we cannot stop in that kindergarten halfway house. If the Providence of God is no more than an occasional incursion of goodness into our life, what becomes of us in the intervals? What insures the permanency of God's favor if in the intervals his wisdom, power and goodness are withdrawn? If, looking at the dark shadows that fall on human life, and looking at the committal with which I have committed myself to him, I could believe that at the minutest point God could let my life slip from his grasp, then it is in him to let my life slip at the supreme point, and I have no Saviour!

A wife made a mistake in the sickroom, gave her husband something else than the medicine intended, and the mistake cost her husband his life. Her reason tottered, and my father went to help her in her despair. "Do you believe," he asked, "that God had the power to prevent you from making the mistake from the results of which you are suffering?"

She had the faith of a Christian and answered, "Oh, yes. I believe that he had."

"Then," my father continued, "if God had the power to keep you from making that mistake, but did not use that power and prevent you, must it not have been for some reason which justified itself to his perfect love and wisdom, and which will justify itself someday to yours?"

In a flash the afflicted woman saw it, and both her reason and her faith were saved.

What is it, after all, that we most desire—to skim the surface of life like butterflies, sipping its honeys, luxuriating in its sunshine, but knowing nothing of the profound experiences by which humanity is instructed and purified and on which alone the everlasting things are built? It is *unto education* that ye endure! The time is coming when we shall thank God from our deepest hearts not only for honey and sunshine, but for the clouds and the bitterness with which he dared to entrust us.

I saw a young man cut down by cancer in a career which the world called success. "Nothing"—these were his words— "nothing but just what has come to me would ever have brought me to my senses. To have found God is worth it all. Prosperity never does anything for us. It is only affliction that makes us, and I am glad for all that has happened." A notation was found after his death as follows: "There is no way of distinguishing between a blessing and a misfortune while it is happening."

In my home town when I was a boy there was a man who exerted a powerful religious influence over us all. But as time passed, he seemed selected for trouble. Though at an undiscerning age myself, I remember how business failure shook him. Then, as in the life of Job, loss followed loss, and sorrow followed sorrow. But when I came back home after an absence of many years, I found him in the prayer-service of the church with his fellow-Christians. He stood and spoke, and I marveled. He seemed like a great, symmetrical oak, whose roots every blast of the tempest had driven deeper, and whose leaves the last rays of the sun were touching with indescribable glory. "Tribulation" had wrought "patience; and patience, experience; and experience, hope."[20] Enduring "as seeing him who is invisible,"[21] he stood there "more than the conqueror."[22] Like Job, he was given to see "the end of the Lord, how that the Lord is full of pity, and merciful."[23]

Only one question really concerns us—are we wholly the Lord's? Then—

"Who shall separate us from the love of Christ? shall tribulation, or anguish, or persecution, or famine, or nakedness, or peril, or sword? Even as it is written, For thy sake we are killed all the day long; We were accounted as sheep for the slaughter. Nay, in all these things we are more than conquerors through him that loved us. For I am persuaded, that neither death nor life, nor angels, nor principalities, nor things present, nor things to come, nor powers, nor height, nor depth, nor any other creature, shall be able to separate us from the love of God, which is in Christ Jesus our Lord."[24]

Prayer and Life's Supreme Joy:
The Prayer of Communion

"He that sent me is with me; he hath not left me alone; for I do always the things that are pleasing to him."

John 8:29 (A. R. V.)

"Behold, the hour cometh, yea, is come, that ye shall be scattered, every man to his own, and shall leave me alone: and yet I am not alone, because the Father is with me."

John 16:32 (A. R. V.)

"Believe me that I am in the Father, and the Father in me."

John 14:11 (A. R. V.)

7

THERE is a prayer nowhere found among the prayers of our great Exemplar, though it abounds among the prayers of his followers, and should abound yet more. It is the Prayer of Confession. "Holy, harmless, undefiled, separate from sinners"[1] as Jesus was, he had nothing to confess. He could challenge and silence his accusers with a word, saying, "Which of you convicteth me of sin?"[2] Jesus "knew no sin,"[3] not from moral blindness, but because there was none in him to know. Such was the testimony of the Father at the baptism, when the heavens were opened, and a voice was heard, saying, "Thou art my beloved Son, in thee I am well pleased."[4]

1.

As only the pure in heart see God, purity of heart and perfection of obedience in Jesus kept him ever in his Father's presence, and made possible the glowing atmosphere out of which all his prayers took their rise. Deep down underneath the Prayers of Self-dedication, of Dependence and Intercession, of Thanksgiving and Submission, lay this perpetual oneness of perfect communion. Fountains of realization were there; reservoirs of strength; rest-times, too, intervening between mighty works, when, kept in perfect peace, his spirit reflected heavenly and divine things as a sheltered Alpine lake reflects the sky; times when no dire evil was threatening and no immediate task beckoning, and Jesus simply sought, found and rested in the bosom of his Father. Thus we learn from Jesus that right relation-

105

ship is the prime necessity, and that we pray joyfully and effectually only as he brings us into harmonious fellowship with God. "The only begotten Son who is in the bosom of the Father"[5] shows us where all true prayer must start.

2.

Years ago, when Mr. Moody was in his prime, I heard him at Northfield tell how one day, sitting in his study, he heard a knock at the door. "Come in," he said. A small boy appeared. "Well, my son, what is it you want?" "I don't want anything," came the answer; "I just wanted to be with you." Then the father of that boy went on to tell of the many, many Christians who, if they ever come to God at all, come simply and solely "to get something out of him," as Mr. Moody put it; Christians who know nothing of the Prayer of Fellowship and Communion, or of the joy, peace and power that flow from it.

A distinguished Christian leader and friend of mine and his small son, away from home overnight, were occupying separate beds in the same room. "E——, you seem restless. Is anything troubling you?"

"Father," came the answer, "is your face turned toward me?"

"Yes, my son." And immediately, the boy was asleep. So in our relationship with God, the need of the child and the longing of the heavenly Parent meet and are satisfied in the Prayer of Fellowship and Communion.

3.

It seems hardly necessary to remark that the Prayer of Fellowship and Communion is a precious and a very necessary kind of prayer. Praying, especially in an intercessory way, is a costly exercise, and will be attended with unnecessary additional strain unless we are blessed with that consciousness of the divine presence and favor which makes all prayer, of whatever kind, instinctive, confident and effectual. Here, as everywhere else, Jesus is our perfect model.

Glints of the intimate communion that bound Jesus to his Father are scattered through the Gospel story. Early in John's Gospel, I read:

"The Son can do nothing of himself, but what he seeth the Father doing: . . . as I hear, I judge."[6]

Startling immediacy, that! We, for our part, seem rather to grope and feel our way. "I feel moved, weighing all considerations, to think or do thus and so," we say. Jesus said, "I see. I hear." But is he not inviting us into an intimacy like his own with the Father when he says:

"My Father and your Father, my God and your God"?[7]

Or when he makes the amazing promise:

"In that day ye shall know that I am in my Father, and ye in me, and I in you"?[8]

4.

If the Bible record is credible, this intimacy of fellowship and communion has from the beginning been the distinguishing mark of God's true children. Back in its earliest pages I read:

"And Enoch walked with God: and he was not, for God took him."[9]

To that astonishing statement a New Testament author adds an astonishing comment:

"For he [Enoch] hath had witness borne to him that before his translation he had been well-pleasing unto God."[10]

Walking with God, then, pleases God! Truly, the supreme wonder of this amazing universe is not its vastness, nor its complexity, nor the lawful interaction of its myriad parts, nor its immeasurable age, nor its mysterious future, but rather this, that the Creator and Upholder of it all desires, prepares the way for, and invites fellowship with his creatures!

The scriptural representation of God as a "jealous"[11] God is an offensive and ignorant anthropomorphism to some. Is this not, however, tragic superficiality? If there is one thing above others that we should adore God for on our knees it is this, that he, the Changeless Fountain of all good and the Sole Hope of humankind, cannot endure that we should set our affections on anything outside himself.

What means the admonition:

"But know that Jehovah hath set apart for himself him that is godly"?[12]

The psalmist himself, enraptured, supplies the answer:

"In thy presence is fulness of joy; in thy right hand there are pleasures for evermore. . . . with thee is the fountain of life. . . . Whom have I in heaven but thee? And there is none on earth that I desire besides thee. My flesh and my heart faileth; but God is the strength of my heart and my portion for ever."[13]

"God," said John Donne in a sermon, "is like us in this also, that he takes it worse to be slighted, to be neglected, to be left out, than to be actually injured. Our inconsideration, our not thinking of God in our actions, offends him more than our sins." And that ancient and incomparable saint, Launcelot Andrewes, in an evening prayer that he draws up for a family in his *Holy Devotions,* makes them all say: "We have fled from thee seeking us: we have neglected thee loving us: we have stopped our ears against thee speaking to us: we have forgotten thee doing good to us: we have despised thee correcting us."

The Book of Psalms extols this fellowship. The twenty-third, or Shepherd Psalm, is the best-loved exposition of it. The one hundred nineteenth is the longest, most yearning cry for it. The entire Old Testament, summed up, is an invitation to it. Of this let one of its last words assure us:

"He hath shewed thee, O man, what is good; and what doth the Lord require of thee, but to do justly, and to love mercy, and to walk humbly with thy God?"[14]

5.

It is as we turn the pages of the New Testament, however, that the potentialities of this fellowship of men with God open up most widely.

"And he appointed twelve, that they might be with him, and that he might send them forth."[15]

That was the only theological seminary these first disciples had, or needed. The Son of God walked with them, ate with them, reasoned with them, rejoiced with them, suffered and endured with them.

"No longer do I call you servants; for the servant knoweth not what his lord doeth: but I have called you friends; for all things that I heard from my Father I have made known unto you."[16]

He sought the solace of their companionship, vainly, in the hour of his agony in the Garden. And how he hastened to them after the resurrection—to Peter and James, to the Emmaus travelers, to the women; for crucifixion and burial, resurrection and ascension, had no power to bring to an end this fellowship between earth and heaven.

"I know him whom I have believed . . . At my first defence no one took my part, but all forsook me. . . . But the Lord stood by me, and strengthened me,"[17]

so Paul testifies. And John, exiled on Patmos, relays to us this word of his Master's:

"Behold, I stand at the door, and knock: if any man hear my voice, and open the door, I will come in to him, and will sup with him, and he with me."[18]

John's head once leaned on Jesus' breast; yet he never looks back on those vanished days as to a golden age, but years after says,

"Our fellowship *is* with the Father, and with his Son Jesus Christ."[19]

6.

In this day of universal calamity and vast opportunity, when men are fainting for the sight of one of the promised days of the Son of man, what does the Church of Christ so need as a reviving and renewing of this transforming experience of the divine fellowship? In the biography of Dr. Dale, British theologian and preacher, I read that toward the middle of his public ministry, he "made the discovery that Jesus was alive," and it transformed everything for him. God once said to Hudson Taylor, founder of the China Inland Mission, "I will evangelize inland China through you, if you will walk with me." Spurgeon, the great London preacher, said that he doubted if in forty years he had passed fifteen waking minutes without an experience of fellowship with Jesus Christ. Then that hymn of the faith sings solidest fact:

"Thou, O Christ, art all I want;
More than all in thee I find."

Christ is the "pearl of great price,"[20] the "treasure hid in a field"[21]—hid, alas, from so many. He is the "bright and morning star,"[22] and it is amazing how the dark, ill-omened birds of doubt and fear flap their wings and vanish when his face appears. As dear old Andrew Bonar put it: "We do not need new swords, new spears, new arms. We only need more eye-salve, to see who is on our side."

How a well-intentioned person can grope and stumble until an actual experience with Christ floods the mind with intelligence! At the close of a summer college Y.W.C.A. conference, a young girl came to me in distress. Though nominally Christian, she was utterly at sea. She hardly seemed to believe in Christ as an historical personage, though she might have known that from the Roman historians as well as from the New Testament. When she had talked herself out, I opened the Gospel of John to the fourteenth chapter and read to her this promise:

"He that hath my commandments, and keepeth them, he it is that loveth me; and he that loveth me shall be loved of my Father, and I will love him, and will manifest myself to him."[23]

"Is not that what you need—a revelation?" I asked her. "Yes," she replied, "that is what I need." I never saw her again. I never knew whether she fulfilled the Lord's condition; but I know that if she fulfilled it, Jesus fulfilled his promise and made himself known to her.

I knew a young minister who once lived in a distinctively theological world. Blessed with a theologian for a father, the power to cast the facts of the Christian faith into intellectual moulds and then to build these stones into a symmetrical cathedral of persuasive truth stood before him as his main task and the supreme desideratum. The materials for the structure, gathered from Holy Scripture

and from life, had been established in experience. To
acknowledge them sincerely was to believe. To conform
to them in behavior was to be a Christian. To propagate
them was to be a minister or missionary, and to do this
faithfully and unselfishly was to be a good minister of
Jesus Christ. So, armed with a full quiver of theological
symbols and doctrines, this earnest young man set out to
convert souls and build up a church.

It hardly occurred to him at that early date that, long
on theology, he was short on religious experience. He had
not yet grasped the fact that but for someone's experience of the divine, all that theology talks about never
could have been; that chosen men first, in moments of
illumination, were given to see things which others had
not seen—things that convicted them of sin, prostrated
them in humility, lifted them into penitence and established them in faith; and that only then, endowed with
unquestioned personal spiritual knowledge, had they
shaped their experience into symbolic phrase to clarify
it to themselves and to commend it to others.

He had not in those days grasped the fact that *Christianity is a communicated life,* whose realities are not ap-
prehended by the intellect from the outside but by the
heart and life from the inside. That monumental word
of Jesus to Nicodemus, the Jewish theologian—

"Except a man be born again, he cannot see the kingdom of
God"[24]—

had not yet dawned on him.

Disinclined to find the trouble inside himself, he turned
his criticism on the definitions and symbols. They were
human and imperfect. Inherited from the past, they needed

revision. A more reasoned interpretation of the Bible and
a more "scientific" interpretation of life, he began to think,
might hold the truth which his ministry lacked and his
nature craved. So he read copiously in "advanced" theological and biblical literature, and some of his friends
began to class him with the free-lancers. Working with
an earnestness that told on his strength to commend to
the church over which Providence had placed him such
scant truth as he possessed, his health began to suffer.
There were fountains of wisdom, but he could not tap
them; reservoirs of strength, but he could not draw from
them. He lost his New Testament, for the wonders it
promised to simple faith were not his, and the miracles
there described had no analogue in his own experience.

But when failure and despair began to flap their black
wings above him, what happened? Did God leave him to
grope and flounder on? Not so. In this crisis of danger
he was brought, by God's good grace, into the company of
a group of men whose faces were aglow with an inner joy
and certitude such as he never before had witnessed. They
were like Enoch of old, walking with God, knowing his
will, and doing it from the heart. They seemed living ex-
positions of John's First Epistle: "We know that we know
him"; "We know that we are in him"; "We know that, we
shall be like him"; "We know that we have passed from
death unto life"; "We know that we are of the truth";
"We know that we have the petitions which we have
desired of him"; "We know that he has given us of his
Spirit"; "We know that we are of God."[25]

Those men semed to live with Jesus on the Mount of
Transfiguration, and the sight of them at first threw the
young man back on himself in despair, till one evening,

out alone under the stars, he suddenly found himself face
downward on the ground. It was involuntary, utterly. At
last he was where he long before ought to have been. How
long he lay there he did not know, but when he stood up,
everything was changed. He knew he should never again
be what he had been. Light began to dawn. His New
Testament, which he seemed to have lost, was given back
to him, for now the supernatural no longer disturbed him—
he was experiencing it. And one evening, on a lonely hill,
bright with moonlight, Christ came out of the shadows.
He heard no voice, he saw no form, but in his deepest
self he knew that Christ was real, and stood in actual, felt
relationship to his spirit. Later, while reading the central
chapters of John's Gospel, which teach about the Holy
Spirit, he found the key to it all: Christ was real, Christ
was glorious, *for it was the Spirit that had revealed him!*[26]

The Spirit, the Spirit—there was the secret! Till then
that had been mere "theology" to him, and puzzling theology. He was confused by those central chapters of John's
Gospel. Jesus had promised there to send his disciples
"another Comforter," "the Spirit of truth," to serve as a
more than adequate personal substitute for himself, and to
be with them forever; and then he had said:

"Ye see *me* . . . *I* will not leave you comfortless: *I* will come to
you."[27]

"Well, which?" he found himself asking. "Are there, then
two manifestations, one of Jesus, and one of the Holy
Spirit? Or is there only one, and is the Holy Spirit simply
Jesus appearing invisibly?"

A visit to a moving picture at that time might have gone
far toward relieving his difficulty. In a movie, one faces

a screen upon which a picture is projected. The screen
does not produce the picture. It is produced by an agent
and instrument hid away somewhere. One does not concern onself with agent and instrument unless the film
breaks or the focusing is imperfect; yet without the func-
tioning of agent and instrument there would be no picture. And is not the ministry of the Holy Spirit essentially
similar? "He shall not speak from himself,"[28] Jesus said.
We are only inferentially conscious of the Spirit as operating; we are immediately conscious of the result of his opera-
tion.

A humble washerwoman attended a session of one of the
Keswick conventions. The Ministry of the Holy Spirit had
been the subject of the discussion, and she was going away
disheartened. A more deeply taught listener asked where
lay her trouble.

"Oh," she replied, "I came with the hope of gaining
an experience of the Holy Spirit, and I have not gained it."

"But have you gained anything? Have you become happily conscious of anything?"

"Why, yes," she replied, "I have become very happily
conscious of the presence of the Lord Jesus."

"But that," said the other, "is just the work of the Holy
Spirit, and the final proof that the Holy Spirit is in your
heart. He glorifies the Lord Jesus, makes him a bright
reality to your spirit; he takes the things that belong to
Christ and shows them to you, so that, as you become aware
of these things, you know that he, the Spirit is within."
That woman had come expecting to see the Agent and
Instrument, but she went away content when she learned
that it was that very divine Agent who had filmed the
picture of the living Jesus on her heart.

7.

Nestling on the edge of the edge of the Park, well out
Fifth Avenue in New York City, is the Metropolitan
Museum. Humanity flows past it in strong tide on a fine
Sunday afternoon, and tiny rivulets trickle inside to enjoy
its treasures. Many who never mounted its steps know
that there are treasures there—antique furniture, statuary,
famous pictures, old armor, Assyrian monuments, Greek
and Roman antiquities. They know this not by firsthand
knowledge—only by hearsay. Yet even they know more
than those others who only guess that there must be something there—else why should people drift in, and on occasion even pay admission?

So, centuries ago, multitudes drifted past three crosses
erected on Golgotha. Some mocked, some shrugged their
shoulders, some wept. There may have been among them
pious Jews who were "waiting for the consolation of
Israel," Jews who that very morning had read in the fifty-
third chapter of Isaiah the divine promise of a suffering
Saviour; but when the last cry of the central Sufferer had
been heard, and the soldier's spear had done its work,
and the black darkness had shut everything in, how many
knew what heaven was suffering, and what the God of all
grace was there enacting?

We open and close our Bibles. We file into and out of
church. Led blindfold through a series of religious forms,
we recite prayers and creeds, we sing hymns and we give
gifts. The symbols of the Christian faith are often on our
lips. We use them as the small change of the spiritual
realm. Knowledge of the Christian religion—do we not
possess it? We know there is a Trinity, a most sacred

Cross, and an indispensable and indestructible Church to spread the knowledge of these things to the ends of the earth; but how many of us can with honesty say as a friend of mine, who had suffered bitterly for his faith and triumphed gloriously, once said to me: "John, there are a lot of things I don't know, BUT I KNOW GOD!" And he spoke truly, for it was his prayer—just the listening to it in that Rescue Mission in New York City to which I referred in Chapter 1—that saved a life, transported a carefree, self-sufficient lawyer into Christ's new spiritual world, and through books precipitated by his conversion, made that man in turn a savior of others.

Book-knowledge, knowledge through symbols, knowledge by hearsay, is hollow, ghostly knowledge. It does not fructify the mind or subdue and satisfy the heart. It is without authority. It has nothing to communicate. I go into a quiet, empty room, sing a note, and as I listen, what is the faint note given back to me? The note of the piano, whose strings were alert to the musical vibrations I set in motion when I sang, and which answer back with the identical note I sang. So in the days of his flesh, Jesus spoke and susceptible souls responded. Shaped at creation as by a pre-established harmony to vibrate to the truth he spoke and was, they discerned on the instant Jesus' first-hand knowledge of divine things, and without persuasion or argument surrendered to them, saying, "He taught them as one having authority, and not as the scribes."[29] Are we today speaking with authority, or once more as the Scribes?

8.

"But this," someone cries with alarm, "is *Mysticism*." Well, why not? When Sonny mounts the bus and travels

to school it is Transportation. When he eats a good dinner
and feels happy and satisfied afterward it is Assimilation
and Digestion. When he works hard and masters his
lessons it is Education, and when he has been orderly and
obedient and has done his chores it is Remuneration. What
matters it to him *what* it is, *if* it is?

Why let words browbeat us out of the realities and the
necessities of life? But for what lies hid in that misused
word, *Mysticism*, the church would be without a Bible
and the world without a gospel. What twenty centuries of
Christian history have to say is, that through fellowship
with the Lord Jesus Christ men touch the Being whom
faith calls God and he touches them—and that is mysticism.
It is the glory of Christianity personally to know our
Creator, Preserver and Saviour. Results reveal it—sins forgiven, inmost motives transformed, self-will transcended,
and not least, an eloquent witness to spiritual law and
fact—JOY. Religion never becomes contagious till it becomes joyful, and here at last is Joy's crystal fountain.

Clever men, then, have not coined a word to exalt a
mere fancy to the level of a spiritual creed and law: rather,
humanity had from the beginning longed for a higher
fellowship in which it might both lose and find itself, and
God, in the fullness of time and with answering longing,
gave us his Son. Jesus himself exhibited the true *Mysticism*
in its perfection:

"I am not alone, because the Father is with me."[30]

Then, having stamped it as divine, he bequeathed it to all
his faithful followers:

"In that day ye shall know that I am in my Father, and ye in me,
and I in you."[31]

Picturing himself as Bread, as Water, as Light, as Life, as the True Vine in which our ideal humanity is rooted, Jesus offers himself to the world as life's final satisfaction. He is God's "fulness" and humanity's goal.[32] When he comes, bringing the Father with him, the kingdom of heaven dawns on a human heart.

9.

How simple it all is! A child may know it. I once took a boy of twelve out for a walk. It was one of those crisp, fall days when the air is golden, and the leaves crackle delightfully under foot. We had a confidential talk, and prayed; and then I said, "——, I want you to form the habit of prayer, so that when you get into trouble, you will see the way out, and will make straight, true paths to success." "Oh, yes, I do," the lad answered. "When I get into trouble, I pray, and then"—here he made a lifting gesture with both hands that put vivid meaning into his words—"then, *I feel kind of light!*"

How winsome the human product finally becomes under this divine artistry! I once went into the woods camping with a prize-fighter. Dick was champion welter-weight of the Middle West. His arm was a sledge-hammer and he had never lost a battle. Failing to schedule lesser matches, he had once challenged the heavy-weight champion, Fitzsimmons. But one day, when the fights on which livelihood depended were failing to come his way, Dick drifted in a discouraged frame of mind into John Timothy Stone's church in Chicago, and Stone, that greathearted lover of men, got him on his knees, and Dick gave himself to Christ. From that time on Dick wanted not to knock men out but to save them. I would see him in the woods working among the lumbermen; "George," he would report, "is going to be a Christian . . . Harry says he will give his heart to Christ." And as we set out on our camping trip together, Dick leading the way through the birches and spruces and hardwood trees, I saw him lift his eyes to the sky up above the tree-tops, and I heard him say: "In thy presence is fulness of joy; and at thy right hand there are pleasures for evermore."[33]

10.

How near God is!

"Say not in thy heart, Who shall ascend into heaven? (that is, to bring Christ down:) or, Who shall descend into the abyss? (that is, to bring Christ up from the dead.) But what saith it? The word is nigh thee, in thy mouth, and in thy heart: that is, the word of faith, which we preach."[34]

So mediaeval Saint Theresa put it in her *Way of Perfection*:

"We have no need of wings to go in search of him. Let us enter into the solitude and look within us: it is there that he is. God is so near that he hears the slightest whisper of our lips, and the most secret thought. Let us talk with him in great humility, but also with love, like children talking with their Father, confidently telling him our troubles and begging him to help us, and recognizing above all that we are not worthy to bear the name of children."

11.

"I have laid my pipe too short of the fountain!" laments a sainted Scot of long ago. So laments many a soul today. "I prayed once," I hear a voice say, "with all the ardor and simple faith of a child, believing all things, hoping all things, expecting all things. Then something shocked, disappointed, disillusioned me. I stopped praying, for I

found I had stopped believing. I am not happy. I could
say in Thomas Hood's lines:

> 'I remember, I remember
>   The fir trees dark and high;
> I used to think their slender tops
>   Were close against the sky;
> It was a childish ignorance,
>   But now 'tis little joy
> To know I'm further off from heav'n
>   Than when I was a boy.' "

So earnest-hearted Nicodemus reasoned:

"How can a man be born when he is old? can he enter a second
time into his mother's womb, and be born?"—[35]

till Jesus, all grace and all power, responded:

"That which is born of the flesh is flesh; and that which is born
of the Spirit is spirit."[36]

So the prodigal reasoned, till shame and want pressed him
sore, and dreaming of the old home and his Father's love,
he humbly ventured back, to find a loving kiss, a ring,
the best robe and a banquet of joy awaiting him!

There is a man now with God, who when he was with
me here always seemed to have a heavenly mind. Everything I have endeavored to say in this chapter and in
this little book he seemed deeply to know. Whenever we
met, we prayed together; and when he prayed, he often
closed his prayer as I would conclude my thoughts on the
Prayer of Fellowship and Communion, with these words:

*"In the Fellowship of Christ, by the Power of the
Spirit, for the Glory of God."*

INDEX OF BIBLICAL REFERENCES

References from the Authorized Version except those otherwise indicated.

(ASV) —American Standard Version.

6—John 11:41, 42 (ASV)

7—Mark 11:22-24—Marginal reading (ASV)

8—1 John 5:15 (ASV)

9—Luke 22:31, 32

10—Luke 23:34

11—John 17:11, 21 (ASV)

12—John 17:15 (ASV)

13—John 17:24 (ASV)

14—1 John 3:3

15—Ps. 127:2 (ASV)

16—Ps. 4:8 (ASV)

17—Rom. 8:34; Heb. 7:25

18—Col. 4:17

19—Rev. 1:5, 6 (ASV)

20—Ex. 19:6 (ASV)

21—1 John 5:16 (ASV)

22—Matt. 12:32 (ASV)

Chapter 5

1—John 5:19 (ASV)

2—1 Thess. 5:18

3—1 Cor. 1:27-29 (ASV)

4—John 16:24—Author's translation

5—Luke 10:20

6—Luke 10:21

7—Luke 10:22

8—John 14:6

9—John 14:9

10—Isa. 40:18-20

11—Matt. 15:13

12—Ps. 40:5

13—Ps. 50:23

Chapter 6

1—Mark 14:33, 34 (ASV)

2—Luke 22:44 (ASV)

3—Luke 24:25, 26 (ASV)

4—Isa. 53:5

5—John 1:29

6—2 Cor. 5:21 (ASV)

7—Heb. 2:9

8—Ex. 12:8

9—John 11:11 (ASV)

10—Mark 5:39 (ASV)

11—Mark 15:34

12—Heb. 5:7 (ASV)

13—Rom. 8:32

14—Matt. 27:42

15—1 Tim. 1:15

16—1 Tim. 1:14

17—Rom. 12:2

18—1 John 4:8

19—Luke 12:7

20—Rom. 5:3, 4

21—Heb. 11:27

22—Rom. 8:37

23—James 5:11 (ASV)

24—Rom. 8:35-39 (ASV)

Chapter 7

1—Heb. 7:26

2—John 8:46 (ASV)

3—2 Cor. 5:21

4—Mark 1:11 (ASV)

5—John 1:18 (ASV)

6—John 5:19, 30 (ASV)

7—John 20:17 (ASV)

8—John 14:20

9—Gen. 5:24

10—Heb. 11:5 (ASV)

11—Ex. 20:5

12—Ps. 4:3 (ASV)

13—Ps. 6:11; 36:9; 73:25, 26 (ASV)

14—Mic. 6:8

15—Mark 3:14 (ASV)

16—John 15:15 (ASV)

17—2 Tim. 1:12; 4:16, 17 (ASV)

18—Rev. 3:20

19—1 John 1:3

20—Matt. 13:46